Rafael Alberti

THE OTHER SHORE

100 Poems by Rafael Alberti

Edited by Kosrof Chantikian

Translated by
José A. Elgorriaga & Martin Paul

Introduction by Gabriel Berns

KOSMOS
San Francisco
1981

Works in Spanish copyright © 1961, 1967, 1977, 1978, and 1979
by Rafael Alberti and are reprinted in this edition with his kind
consent.

Some of these translations first appeared in *Portland Review,
Ironwood, KOSMOS, Quarterly West, Backwash* and *American
Poetry Review.*

Library of Congress Catalog Card Number: 80-84602
ISBN: 0-916426-05-X (cloth)
0-916426-06-8 (paper)

MODERN POETS IN TRANSLATION SERIES
(Volume I)

This project was supported partially by funding from
the National Endowment for the Arts.

KOSMOS
381 Arlington Street
San Francisco, CA 94131
USA

CONTENTS

Contents (continued):

Contents (continued):

Contents (continued):

PREFACE

The Spanish text as presented here—because no one de-
finitive edition yet exists for the works of Rafael Alberti—is
taken from three different editions: *Poesías Completas* (Buenos
Aires: Editorial Losada, 1961); *Poesía (1924-1967)* (Madrid:
Aguilar, 1972); and Alberti's complete works recently pub-
lished in sixteen separate paperback volumes by Seix Barral
(Barcelona, 1977-80).

Various discrepancies exist between these three editions
such as stanza breaks, misspellings and accents missing or mis-
placed—the latter especially in the Aguilar edition in words
such as "sólo" ("only") and "solo" ("alone") (see for example,
pp. 168-69). I've made a careful comparison of each poem
from these different texts in an attempt to determine how
Alberti meant his poems to be. I am very grateful to Gabriel
Berns for his suggestions in helping me to answer these
questions.

José Elgorriaga and Martin Paul must be greatly thanked
for their close collaboration in producing these translations.

Disagreements—are they not inevitable when more than
one of us is involved in the birth and nourishment of poems
from one language to another? Probably certain differences
still exist between us: majority opinion in such situations does
nothing for the authenticity, the integrity of the poem as a
new work, a work *re-created* in English. Each of us defended
passionately our own intuitions on behalf of the half-dozen
or so English poems over which we could not easily see eye
to eye. We also listened to one another. And in that empty
space between argument and acceptance, reflection and still-
ness, these translations, these *transformations,* were born.

—*K. C.*
San Francisco
January 1981

FOREWORD

Modern, as I use it in the title for this series *(Modern Poets in Translation)* does not imply simply "new" or "recent" or "original." If Picasso is modern, then so are Blake and Beethoven. If Baudelaire and Whitman, then Copernicus. No. It is not simply the "new" which is modern; something else—some pervasive element running through the works of these artists makes them modern for us: an unrelenting ingredient of transfiguration and regeneration which severs, absorbs and continues itself, which shatters, heals and then embraces itself and that emptiness from which it came—the reflection of its own gaze. The distinguishing element of the modern poem is *negation, criticism:* the power of the modern poem exists in so far as these two elements (which are identical) exist. The modern poem is also paradox, contradiction: to *negate* is to destroy, transmute, but at the same time to *continue,* the past, the world, history.

A love poem by Sappho is a *work,* it is *living.* The modern poem is always more: it too lives but in a radically different way: it is language face to face with itself, language which rips off the mask of chatter to find that *otherness* in the world—*You.* Critical of the history into which it was born and conscious of the necessity to transmute, to transfigure this history into true reality—the *Present*—modern poetry is the regeneration of time as *presence:* this *moment, now, here, with you.*

The poem is rupture, a break in the suffocating chain of history. The modern poem is rupture and simultaneously continuation and renewal of the past. Born into the continuum of history, the poet celebrates the attempt to annul history, or at least to neutralize it, to re-create it—by returning to the beginning of beginnings, the origin of the world, return to that time when the Word was unfettered, unfragmented, when dichotomies did not exist, when Freedom & Action were inseparable.

If the infinite echo of that mutation we call *history,* its inertia of silence, residing in our minds and pockets makes us

walk slower than we would like, dissolving the living shadows
of our breath, our movement, annuling the reveries of the
touching skin; if laughter is made cripple because of the
shroud history causes to loom above and beneath our stare,
our look; and if the imagination sings with a tongue deformed
and contaminated by the barbed wire of "progress," then we
have a right to ask: How much is it possible to transmute this
history, to metamorphosize the mutilation of our senses into
a planetary sensibility, to *become what we may be: to Invent
Ourselves?*

   This question and the insinuation it simultaneously gives
birth to are present in the work of the modern poet. The poem,
unlike prose, does not attempt to *explain* the world, it *re-
creates* it. This means stripping history bare into its real form:
time. Time in the poem is the instantaneous present, here,
now.* Time as presence is the poem. The modern poem:
language as intentionality, image, analogy: negation, criticism:
language as movement toward itself, its shadow in perpetual
pursuit of that otherness in the world—the *You*; language as
its own death and unending rebirth.

   If, for Baudelaire, the poem is the analogy of the uni-
verse, it must be because the poem, through its own energy,
its own directive, continually destroys and re-creates history:
time. The poem does this by annuling at the velocity of light
the expansion and recession of history, of "progress," and
therefore time.

   Sappho and Dante are not *modern* in the sense I have
just outlined because their works exist in *uncritical* time. For
the ancients time was, as Aristotle believed, periodic, cyclical,
everlasting circular motion. The winged hound of Zeus would
devour each day the liver of Prometheus—Aeschylus tells us.
Beginning with St. Augustine, this Greek conception of circu-
lar time is displaced by an unrelenting, irreversible, rectilinear
movement of history. This would continue, Augustine be-
lieved, for a finite time until that Day of days—Judgment—
brings us eternal, unchanging ecstasy or flails the human skin

---

*To learn to see to hear to say
                    The instantaneous
Is our trade. . . .
                    —Octavio Paz in "Letter to León Felipe"

numb in hell. God will dissolve time; motion will swallow it-
self. There will no longer be death because birth will have
been abolished. It is this concept of time Dante inherits and
out of which he constructs the supreme architecture of his
Divine Comedy.

The modern poem is a criticism, a destruction, a trans-
mutation of everlasting circular time and Christian rectilinear
time into the *Present.* With Blake and the Romantics, Con-
sciousness and the Imagination are reconciled: the poem an-
nounces itself as a progression of contraries: negation and
continuation, history and prophecy, dream and action. Mod-
ern poetry *comprehends time* for the first time in its authen-
tic form: the *Instantaneous Present.* The false mask, once re-
moved, can never again be put on. Energy becomes, is the
same as, Eternal Delight.

                    —Kosrof Chantikian
                    General Editor—*Modern Poets in Translation*
                    San Francisco, January 1981

POETRY AND EXILE – NOT LETTING GO
by
Gabriel Berns

The rose and the archangel had not been born.
It was the time before the bleating and tears
when light still did not know
if the sea would be male or female,
when wind dreamed of long hair to comb
and fire dreamed of cheeks and carnations to burn
and water of lips stopping to drink.
It was before the body, before name and time.

It was then, I remember, that once long ago, in heaven . . .

          —Rafael Alberti
           from "Three Memories of Heaven"

I

Rafael Alberti is a poet of many voices. There is, however, a leitmotif of longing that is heard again and again in his works, a theme conveyed so delicately in the opening lines of his "Tres recuerdos del cielo" ("Three Memories of Heaven"). It strives to capture the poet's feelings of nostalgia for a lost paradise, for a time prior to Creation: ". . . before the bleating and tears / when light still did not know / if the sea would be male or female." This prevalent emotional response is clearly related to Alberti's sense and experience of exile, as well as to his unwillingness to allow his childhood past and its accompanying innocence to fade from memory. But in spite of the recurrence of this theme in so many of Alberti's poems, his poetry is not in the least monochromatic or monotonous. On the contrary, it remains richly varied in scope and tonality.

Alberti has written almost mythical and certainly magical poetry inspired by his beloved Mediterranean and its sandy beaches near his birthplace in southern Spain; he has composed haunting folk ballads and songs which touch intimately on the ancient traditions of Andalucía, Spain's most Arabic-influenced and exotic region; he has written poems describing the architectural monuments and the frequently stark

1

countryside from Madrid north to the rugged coastal areas on
the Bay of Biscay; he has created works in the classical mode
as well as in a quasi-surrealistic style; and he has even success-
fully captured the flavor and spirit of the silent film era in a
series of highly original poems about Buster Keaton, Charlie
Chaplin, and Harold Lloyd. His own dedication to painting
and drawing led him to write a group of ambitious poems de-
voted to the world's most famous painters, gathering them
together under the reverential title of *A la pintura (To Paint-
ing)*. Rafael Alberti's complete works include poetry on China,
France, Russia, Argentina and Italy, countries which he either
visited briefly or where he lived for extended periods of time
during his nearly forty years of exile from Spain. Unfortu-
nately, he was not totally immune from writing circumstantial
and at times strident political poetry, most of which came into
being during the early years of the Spanish Civil War when
Alberti considered himself to be "un poeta en la calle," a poet
of the streets, in the service of the Spanish revolution. He
composed a series of poems to honor his friend and fellow
exile, Pablo Picasso, on the artist's eighty-ninth birthday–*Los
8 nombres de Picasso (The 8 Names of Picasso)*–a collection
which Alberti managed to have published in Spain in 1970,
while the country was still firmly under Francisco Franco's
grip and tight censorship. His latest book of poems, *Fustigada
luz (Driven Light)* published in Barcelona in 1980, contains
poems written from 1972 to 1978 and is a work of great
breadth and variety. It includes ballads, elegies to fellow poets
and artists, twenty-two poems and accompanying calligraphic
sketches (by Alberti) dedicated to the art of Joan Miró, poems
on Neruda as well as one addressed to the assassinated Presi-
dent of Chile, Salvador Allende, and a final long, autobiograph-
ical poetic sketch which bears the delightful title "Denuestos y
alabanzas rimadas en mi propio honor" ("Insults and Rhymed
Words of Praise in Honor of Me"). The entire book consti-
tutes a representative Albertian display of exuberance and al-
most manic playfulness which belies the poet's seventy-eight
years. The many voices of Rafael Alberti succeed in coming
together here to form a singular, harmonious blend.

II

It seems to me that an interesting and elucidating comparison can be made between Pablo Picasso and Rafael Alberti. There is a torrential quality about Alberti's creative activity which is clearly to be found in the works of Picasso, and it was not merely coincidence nor the circumstances arising from the Civil War in Spain which brought these two very Spanish artists together in friendship. The Spanish critic Manuel Durán has written about the inevitability of comparing the poetic style of Alberti with the painting techniques of Picasso. For Durán, Picasso and Alberti are both moralists of our time who have been able to domesticate their own personal demons, thus leading the way for others to do the same. To my mind, it is the almost constant display of exuberant vitality, the sense of never being at rest, which makes it inevitable that a reader of Alberti's poetry would compare it to the works of this other prolific Andalusian artist. It is, I think, highly significant that Alberti himself wrote several prose pieces describing a series of visits which he made to Picasso in the southern French village of Mougins during the period from 1968 to 1972. One of the earliest of these diary-like entries offers us Alberti's unusual reactions to various sketches which Picasso showed him:

> Picasso shows me his most recent drawings: two enormous portfolios filled with them. They are line drawings of nude figures, impeccable, truly erotic obsessions. Some are terribly powerful, revealing Picasso's constant vital hunger, that fire which perhaps he fears is threatening to become extinguished and which he wishes to keep alive at all costs. They are angry heads, kissing each other frenetically on the lips, biting one another like wild animals, almost to the point of tearing each other apart with their teeth. In the midst of my immense admiration, I felt a profound sadness.

There is an undeniable element of self-portraiture in Alberti's description since *his* poetry on occasion displays this kind of fury, anger and even erotic obsession. But what it does convey above all else, from the earliest poems to his most recent, is that undiminished vitality—exceedingly youthful and almost adolescent in its need to be obsessively stated—expressed with the same economy of means and suggestion so often found in the line drawings and etchings of Picasso. Reading or viewing such works, we come away with the impression they were conceived and executed in sudden, explosively spontaneous bursts of creative energy. There is an immediacy and poetic agility present in most of Alberti's compositions, qualities consistently discovered in much of Picasso's art. At the very center of the artistic philosophy of both men, no matter how protean their stylistic inventions seem to be throughout their long lives, we readily find the need to maintain an innocence and almost primitive open-eyed wonder toward the world, and to express the novelty of this vision in the playful, imaginative and naturally graceful ways of a child. Mixed in with this childlike freshness and abandon, however, is a sense of mischief, of precociousness and even some compulsion to "impress."

Picasso did not outlive Franco and his regime in Spain in spite of his own longevity, but on April 27, 1977 Rafael Alberti finally returned "home" after an absence of almost four decades. On that day hundreds of admirers and reporters were at the airport in Madrid to greet the poet on his arrival from Rome, his most recent place of residence during his long but fruitful exile. Although most of the extensive body of poetry Alberti had written and published outside of Spain had not been readily or, indeed, even legally available to Spanish readers, his name was familiar to many Spaniards, almost as well known as that of Pablo Picasso. More manifestly political in orientation, words, and actions than Picasso, Alberti was seen by many of his countrymen as a living symbol of stubborn survival. His return to Spain for the first time since his departure as a voluntary exile early in 1939 was an event which truly signified the end of that long, repressive regime which had been so detrimental to the artistic and intellectual life of Spain.

Franco was now dead, the new Spain was on its way to re-creating a democratic form of government, and the long diaspora of the Spanish exiles had finally come to an end after having assumed almost biblical proportions and offering a pre-view of what was yet to come during World War II. The re-turning poet, Rafael Alberti, had not only survived the histori-cal events and personal tragedies of the Spanish Civil War and the ensuing flood-like exodus of several hundreds of thousands of refugees, but he had in many ways managed to thrive as a poet and as a citizen of what came to be known as *La España Peregrina*—"Wandering Spain." Alberti's first public words to those on hand to welcome him and his wife, the novelist María Teresa León, on that day in April were: "I have come back to Spain so that I may continue to be the Spaniard I have always been."

The poetry of Rafael Alberti composed in exile is gener-ally retrospective and nostalgically backward-looking. Spain, particularly that region of Spain Alberti knew and experienced so fully as a child, are constantly recalled and re-created in his poetry and his autobiography, *La arboleda perdida (The Lost Grove)*. The poet's lifelong love affair and obsession with the sea, his continual search for light and clarity in his own crea-tive activity, and the graceful, arabesque flow of his poetic line are all related to Alberti's particular brand of "Spanishness" and his buoyant childhood in the Puerto de Santa María, prov-ince of Cádiz, Andalucía.

When Alberti writes about Picasso in the prose sketches already mentioned, he consciously identifies himself with his friend, attributing many of their similar traits as he defines them to their childhood years in Andalucía:

> Picasso was nursed by Andalucía until he was ten years old, and I was not weaned from her until I was over four-teen. He never returned. I have gone back on very rare occasions, for the briefest of visits. To his childhood in Málaga Picasso undoubtedly owes all that light, madness, wit, passion, rapture, capriciousness, that violent playful-ness and jesting. ... In my own case, if I can be excused for comparing myself to him, I owe the full substance of my poetry to the sea of Cádiz.

It seems obvious that those qualities which Alberti ascribes to Picasso and which he apparently admired so much in his

friend's work, are the very qualities Alberti rightly feels consti-
tute the principal elements of his own poetry. In a recent tele-
vision interview in Spain and later in a conversation we had
together, Alberti spoke about his childhood in Puerto de Santa
María and restated his belief that the sea had always been his
maestro, his teacher. Rafael Alberti has also frequently empha-
sized the pursuit of light and clarity in his poetry. In the short
preface to his *Fustigada luz,* he reaffirms this goal:"We see
light in darkness, in the most frightening shadows we can see
it, desire it, thrash about in the darkest underwater cavern in
search of it. Because light is there, always there, up above, on
high, or in the deepest chasm, within everyone's reach.... All
these poems move in the direction of light, even those which
have been most invaded by shadows."

There can be little doubt that both movement and lumi-
nosity are the salient features of Alberti's poetic activity, even
in the darker poems composed during his so-called surrealistic
phase. These same characteristics are also to be found in Al-
berti's lyrical drawings, his *liricografías.* A personal note or a
dedication written by Alberti in one of his books is generally
a full-fledged *liricografía,* an unbroken line forming words that
are quite unexpectedly transformed into sailboats, fish or even
the profile of a guitar. This blending of the visual and the po-
etic word is a frequent phenomenon in his poetry and it comes
as no real surprise to note the poet's deep admiration and affin-
ity for the works of the Catalán painter Joan Miró. Alberti is
very much aware of this fusion in his poetry and he has even
said that he "paints poems." The fluid movement of his po-
etry, however, is not meant to divert or confuse us. It is, on
the contrary, the poet's attempt to create a framework for
clarification and emphasis. In his *Diario de un día (Diary of a
Day),* Alberti wrote a brief description of the process: "The
straight line, quite simple at first, begins to curve on me almost
immediately, weaving in and out in a complex pattern of its
own and forming a labyrinth of turns and returns with no ap-
parent resolution. But each tendril of this complex vine is
clearly defined, creating the structure for an exact design which
simplifies what is obscure, making it luminous."

III

The "Generation of 1927" is the name frequently given to the group of highly talented Spanish poets to which Rafael Alberti belongs. The poetry produced by the members of this literary generation has, according to many critics, given rise to a second Golden Age of Spanish Literature. Included in this group of poets are Federico García Lorca, Jorge Guillén, Luis Cernuda, Pedro Salinas, Vicente Aleixandre, Miguel Hernández and Gerardo Diego. Not all of them have received the international prominence which their works, their poetic inventiveness deserve. Perhaps the most famous of all was García Lorca, whose tragic murder during the early days of the Spanish Civil War was partially responsible for bringing his richly textured poetry to the attention of readers throughout the world. The awarding of the Nobel Prize for Literature to Vicente Aleixandre in 1977 has also undoubtedly had the effect of creating additional interest in Spanish poetry of this century on an international level.

Alberti has often been compared to Lorca, and there can be no doubt at all that Alberti greatly admired this poet from Granada whose works he heard Lorca read in the gardens of the Residencia de Estudiantes in Madrid where so many young Spanish poets, writers and artists, including Dalí and Buñuel, gathered in the early 1930s. Alberti recalls that time and his subsequent, complex relationship with García Lorca in a poem written some fifteen years after Lorca's death, "Retornos de un poeta asesinado" ("The Return of an Assassinated Poet"). Alberti addresses his dead friend who appears to him "in the sleeping / light of a tranquil dream in March," seeing him as he always saw him in life. In a fine example of the special way in which Alberti works with language in his poetry, the lovely gardens of this student residence are richly condensed by the poet into "aquellos jardines de estudiantiles chopos" ("those gardens of student poplars") where Lorca startled and captivated his audience with his recitation of the Gypsy Ballads. Alberti's closeness to Lorca, what has even been suggested by some to be his dependence on him for inspiration, might be summed up in the lines which appear toward the end of this

interesting, tormented poem: "you remain attached to me
more than ever in death / for those times perhaps / we were
not—oh, forgive me!—in life." As I have indicated elsewhere,
Alberti shares with García Lorca a very special approach to
popular or traditional themes and imagery of an Andalucía
that both poets re-created in their respective works. How-
ever, Alberti's poems tend to be more ethereal, more eccen-
tric and even more blithely musical than most of Lorca's
works. As a result, Alberti is even more difficult to translate
than his famous compatriot whose poems have been frequently
transposed into English.

Particularly unique to Alberti among this group of poets
is the way in which he has refused to *let go,* refused to relin-
quish his childhood as he remembers or imagines it to have
been. These memories appear again and again in almost every-
thing he writes, and they continue to sustain Alberti even
years after his physical return to the country of his birth. His
not letting go of this almost inexhaustible vein of poetic in-
spiration has given his poetry a particular poignancy as he
converts scenes and settings from his distant past into pro-
digious landscapes and seascapes of his imagination.

IV

All translations of poetry are doomed to at least one kind
of failure since the sounds of the original poem must inevitably
be modified by the act of framing them within a different lan-
guage, with its *own* special sonic patterns. But it is equally
true that poetry in translation carries within it new harmonies
and chords which have come into the receiving language through
the original work. Poetic translation therefore can be and often
does constitute an enrichment—as listeners or readers we hear
and see things never heard or seen before in our native lan-
guage. To translate, in this way, is to *create.* And successful
translations of poetry offer us a freshness of sound and image
not at all unlike what we derive from the original poem itself.

MARINERO EN TIERRA

[1924]

SAILOR ON LAND

25

Retorcedme sobre el mar,
al sol, como si mi cuerpo
fuera el jirón de una vela.

Exprimid toda mi sangre.
Tended a secar mi vida
sobre las jarcias del muelle.

Seco, arrojadme a las aguas
con una piedra en el cuello
para que nunca más flote.

Le di mi sangre a los mares.
¡Barcos, navegad por ella!
Debajo estoy yo, tranquilo.

25

Wring me out over the sea,
in the sun, as though my body
were the shred of a sail.

Squeeze out all my blood.
Spread my life to dry
over the rigging of the pier.

Once dry, throw me into the water
with a stone around my neck
so that I'll never float again.

I gave my blood to the seas.
Sail through it, ships!
I'm down below, resting.

33

Nací para ser marino
y no para estar clavado
en el tronco de este árbol.

Dadme un cuchillo.

¡Por fin, me voy de viaje!
—¿Al mar, a la luna, al monte?
—¡Qué sé yo! ¡Nadie lo sabe!

Dadme un cuchillo.

33

I was born to be a sailor
and not to be nailed
to the trunk of this tree.

Give me a knife.

At last, I'm going to travel!
"To the sea, to the moon, to the mountain?"
"How do I know! No one knows!"

Give me a knife.

36

LA NIÑA QUE SE VA AL MAR

¡Qué blanca lleva la falda
la niña que se va al mar!

¡Ay niña, no te la manche
la tinta del calamar!

¡Qué blancas tus manos, niña,
que te vas sin suspirar!

¡Ay niña, no te las manche
la tinta del calamar!

¡Qué blanco tu corazón
y qué blanco tu mirar!

¡Ay niña, no te los manche
la tinta del calamar!

36

THE LITTLE GIRL GOING DOWN TO THE SEA

How white the skirt she wears
the little girl going down to the sea!

Oh child, don't let it be stained
by the ink of the squid!

How white your hands, little girl,
as you go by without sighing!

Oh child, don't let them be stained
by the ink of the squid!

How white your heart
and how white your glance!

Oh child, don't let them be stained
by the ink of the squid!

37

DIME QUE SÍ

Dime que sí,
compañera,
marinera,
dime que sí.

Dime que he de ver la mar,
que en la mar he de quererte.
Compañera,
dime que sí.

Dime que he de ver el viento,
que en el viento he de quererte.
Marinera,
dime que sí.

Dime que sí,
compañera,
dime,
dime que sí.

37

SAY IT'S SO

Say it's so,
compañera,
marinera,
say it's so.

Tell me I must see the sea,
that I must want you in the sea.
Compañera,
say it's so.

Tell me I must see the wind,
that I must want you in the wind.
Marinera,
say it's so.

Say it's so,
compañera,
say it,
say it's so.

44

Recuérdame en alta mar,
amiga, cuando te vayas
y no vuelvas.

Cuando la tormenta, amiga,
clave un rejón en la vela.

Cuando alerta el capitán
ni se mueva.

Cuando la telegrafía
sin hilos ya no se entienda.

Cuando ya al palo-trinquete
se lo trague la marea.

Cuando en el fondo del mar
seas sirena.

44

Remember me on the high seas
my love, when you leave
and never return.

When the storm, my love,
drives a spear into the sail.

When the captain on watch
doesn't move.

When the wireless
no longer understands.

When the foremast finally
is swallowed by the waves.

When you are a siren
at the bottom of the sea.

53

¿Qué piensas tú junto al río,
junto al mar que entra en tu río?

—Aquellas torres tan altas,
no sé si torres de iglesias
son, o torres de navío.

—Torres altas de navío.

53

What do you think of by the river,
by the sea that empties into your river?

"Those towers so high,
I don't know if they're church towers
or ship towers."

"High ship towers."

62

Si mi voz muriera en tierra,
llevadla al nivel del mar
y dejadla en la ribera.

Llevadla al nivel del mar
y nombradla capitana
de un blanco bajel de guerra.

¡Oh mi voz condecorada
con la insignia marinera:
sobre el corazón un ancla
y sobre el ancla una estrella
y sobre la estrella el viento
y sobre el viento la vela!

62

If my voice dies on land,
carry it to sea level
and leave it on the shore.

Carry it to sea level
and commission it captain
of a white ship of war.

Imagine my voice decorated
with the mariner's medal:
an anchor over my heart
and upon the anchor a star
and upon the star the wind
and upon the wind the sail!

LA AMANTE
[1925]
THE LOVER

56

Sierra de Pancorbo.

Ya no sé, mi dulce amiga,
mi amante, mi dulce amante,
ni cuales son las encinas,
ni cuales son ya los chopos,
ni cuales son los nogales,
que el viento se ha vuelto loco,
juntando todas las hojas,
tirando todos los árboles.

56

Sierra de Pancorbo

I don't know anymore, my sweet friend,
my love, my sweet love,
which are the oaks,
or which are the poplars,
or which are the walnuts,
since the wind's gone mad,
and gathered all the leaves together,
and knocked down every tree.

EL ALBA DEL ALHELÍ

[1925–1926]

THE DAWN OF THE WALLFLOWER

17

Un duro me dio mi madre,
antes de venir al pueblo,
para comprar aceitunas
allá en el olivar viejo.

Y yo me he tirado el duro
en cosas que son del viento:
un peine, una redecilla
y un moño de terciopelo.

17

My mother gave me a *duro*
before we got to town
to buy olives
at the old olive grove.

And I threw it away
on things made of the wind:
a comb, a hairnet
and a velvet chignon.

3

De arriba, del barrio alto,
vengo por las callejuelas.
Cerrados están los ojos
del pueblo. Todas las puertas
y ventanas tienen clavos.
Traigo
desgarrada la chaqueta.

Temblando,
muerto estoy aquí en tu reja.
Te entrego mi mano, y tú,
en su palma dura y tierna,
le clavas un alfiler
fino, largo y negro,
de cabeza negra.

3

From up there, from the high quarter,
I come down the back streets.
The eyes of the village
are closed. All the doors
and windows nailed up.
I am wearing
my torn vest.

Trembling,
I am dead here at your window.
I give you my hand
and in my hard and tender palm
you stick
a fine, long, black pin,
with a black head.

4

SÚPLICA

(Ya sube las escaleras,
de verde, la primavera.)

—¡Niñas, abrid las ventanas!
Decidle a la carcelera ...

(Ya van aplaudiendo el aire
las palomas mañaneras.)

—¡Palomas de pico blanco,
decidle a la carcelera! ...

(La sombra del calabozo
no siente el azul de afuera.)

—¡Arcángeles de las torres,
decidle a la carcelera! ...

(La ventana de la cárcel
es ventanita de hierro,
por donde no pasa el aire.)

4

ENTREATY

(Already, dressed in green, spring
is coming up the stairs.)

"Open the windows, children!
Tell the jailer, tell her . . ."

(Already the morning doves
are clapping for the air.)

"White-beaked doves,
tell the jailer! . . ."

(The shadow of the prison
doesn't feel the blue outside.)

"Archangels of the towers,
tell the jailer! . . ."

(The window of my cell
is a small iron window
through which no air passes.)

3

Sobre el olivar,
flotando, el amigo
que se fue a la mar.

¿Muerto?
—No, muerto, no.
Desnudo y el pecho abierto,
le veo yo.

Muchachas que vais a Loja,
sobre el olivar vecino,
veréis, flotando, al amigo.

¿Muerto?
—No, muerto, no.
Desnudo y el pecho abierto,
le veo yo.

Sobre el olivar,
sangrando, el amigo
que se fue a la mar.

3

Above the olive grove,
floating, the friend
who went to sea.

Dead?
"No, not dead.
I see him
naked, his chest open."

You girls on the way to Loja,
you will see him, floating,
above the nearby olive grove.

Dead?
"No, not dead.
I see him
naked, his chest open."

Above the olive grove,
bleeding, the friend
who went to sea.

3
TORRE DE IZNÁJAR

Prisionero en esta torre,
prisionero quedaría.

(Cuatro ventanas al viento.)

—¿Quién grita hacia el norte, amiga?
—El río, que va revuelto.

(Ya tres ventanas al viento.)

—¿Quién gime hacia el sur, amiga?
—El aire, que va sin sueño.

(Ya dos ventanas al viento.)

—¿Quién suspira al este, amiga?
—Tú mismo, que vienes muerto.

(Y ya una ventana al viento.)

—¿Quién llora al oeste, amiga?
—Yo, que voy muerta a tu entierro.

¡Por nada yo en esta torre
prisionero quedaría!

3

TOWER OF IZNÁJAR

I want to remain
a prisoner in this tower.

(Four windows to the wind.)

"Who yells to the North, my love?"
"The river, restlessly flowing."

(Three windows left to the wind.)

"Who groans to the South, my love?"
"The air, going without sleep."

(Two windows left to the wind.)

"Who sighs to the East, my love?"
"You, yourself, coming dead."

(And now one window left to the wind.)

"Who cries to the West, my love?"
"I do, coming dead to your burial."

Nothing will keep me now
a prisoner in this tower!

21

Aquellos ojos que vi,
¿dónde están,
que ya no los veo?
¿Dónde los vi?

Tiraban de aquellos ojos
las cuerdas de los cabellos
que me amarraban a mí.

Las cuerdas de los cabellos,
¿dónde están
que ya no las veo?
¿Dónde las vi?

21

Where are they,
those eyes I once saw,
and don't see anymore?
Where did I see them?

The cords of hair
that bound me
unwound from those eyes.

Where are they,
the cords of hair
I don't see anymore?
Where did I see them?

SOBRE LOS ÁNGELES

[1927–1928]

CONCERNING THE ANGELS

DESAHUCIO

Ángeles malos o buenos,
que no sé,
te arrojaron en mi alma.

Sola,
sin muebles y sin alcobas.
deshabitada.

De rondón, el viento hiere
las paredes,
las más finas, vítreas láminas.

Humedad. Cadenas. Gritos.
Ráfagas.

Te pregunto:
¿cuándo abandonas la casa,
dime,
qué ángeles malos, crueles,
quieren de nuevo alquilarla?

Dímelo.

EVICTION

Good or evil angels,
I don't know which,
hurled you into my soul.

Lonely,
without furniture or bedrooms,
empty.

Suddenly, the wind strikes
these walls,
thin glassy sheets.

Dampness. Chains. Screams.
Blasts.

Please:
when you leave this place,
tell me,
what cruel, evil angels
will want to rent it next?

Tell me.

EL ÁNGEL DESCONOCIDO

¡Nostalgia de los arcángeles!
Yo era...
Miradme.

Vestido como en el mundo,
ya no se me ven las alas.
Nadie sabe cómo fui.
No me conocen.

Por las calles, ¿quién se acuerda?
Zapatos son mis sandalias.
Mi túnica, pantalones
y chaqueta inglesa.
Dime quién soy.

Y, sin embargo, yo era...

Miradme.

THE UNKNOWN ANGEL

Nostalgia of the archangels!
I was . . .
Look at me.

Dressed like any other man,
my wings no longer show.
Nobody knows what I was.
They don't remember me.

In the street, who's recognized?
My sandals are shoes.
My tunic, pants
and sports coat.
Tell me who I am.

And, still, I was . . .

Look at me.

JUICIO

¡Oh sorpresa de nieve desceñida,
        vigilante, invasora!
Voces veladas, por robar la aurora,
        te llevan detenida.

Ya el fallo de la luz hunde su grito,
        juez de sombra, en tu nada.
(Y en el mundo una estrella fue apagada.
        Otra, en el infinito.)

JUDGMENT

Oh surprise of snow come loose,
    watchful, invading!
Muffled voices arrest you
    for stealing the dawn.

The sentence of the light already drowns his scream,
    judge of shadow, in your nothingness.
(And in the world a star was extinguished.
    Another, in the infinite.)

EL ÁNGEL DE LOS NÚMEROS

Vírgenes con escuadras
y compases, velando
las celestes pizarras.

Y el ángel de los números,
pensativo, volando
del 1 al 2, del 2
al 3, del 3 al 4.

Tizas frías esponjas
rayaban y borraban
la luz de los espacios.

Ni sol, luna, ni estrellas,
ni el repentino verde
del rayo y el relámpago,
ni el aire. Sólo nieblas.

Vírgenes sin escuadras,
sin compases, llorando.

Y en las muertas pizarras,
el ángel de los números,
sin vida, amortajado
sobre el 1 y el 2,
sobre el 3, sobre el 4 . . .

THE ANGEL OF NUMBERS

Virgins with squares
and compasses, watching over
the heavenly blackboards.

And the angel of numbers,
pensive, flying
from 1 to 2, from 2
to 3, from 3 to 4.

Cold chalk and sponges
crossed out and erased
the heavenly lights.

No sun, moon, no stars,
no sudden green
of lightning and thunder,
no air. Only fog.

Virgins without squares
or compasses, crying.

And on the dead blackboards,
the angel of numbers,
lifeless, in a shroud
on the 1 and the 2,
on the 3, on the 4 . . .

CANCÍON DEL ÁNGEL SIN SUERTE

Tú eres lo que va:
agua que me lleva,
que me dejará.

Buscadme en la ola.

Lo que va y no vuelve:
viento que en la sombra
se apaga y se enciende.

Buscadme en la nieve.

Lo que nadie sabe:
tierra movediza
que no habla con nadie.

Buscadme en el aire.

SONG OF THE UNLUCKY ANGEL

You are what moves:
water that takes me,
that will leave me.

Look for me in the wave.

What leaves and never returns:
wind that in shadow
dies down and flares up.

Look for me in the snow.

What no one knows:
drifting earth
that speaks with no one.

Look for me in the air.

EL ÁNGEL DESENGAÑADO

Quemando los fríos,
tu voz prendió en mí:
ven a mi país.

Te esperan ciudades,
sin vivos ni muertos,
para coronarte.

—Me duermo.
No me espera nadie.

THE DISILLUSIONED ANGEL

Burning through cold, your voice
kindled a spark in me:
Come to my country.

Cities, free
of the living and dead,
await you with a crown.

"I'm falling asleep.
No one waits for me."

EL ÁNGEL ÁNGEL

Y el mar fue y le dio un nombre
y un apellido el viento
y las nubes un cuerpo
y un alma el fuego.

La tierra, nada.

Ese reino movible,
colgado de las águilas,
no la conoce.

Nunca escribió su sombra
la figura de un hombre.

THE ANGEL ANGEL

And the sea went and gave her a name
and the wind a surname
and the clouds a body
and fire a soul.

Earth, nothing.

That drifting kingdom
hanging from eagles
doesn't know her.

Her shadow never wrote
the figure of a man.

ENGAÑO

Alguien detrás, a tu espalda,
tapándote los ojos con palabras.

Detrás de ti, sin cuerpo,
sin alma.
Ahumada vox de sueño
cortado.
Ahumada voz
cortada.

Con palabras, vidrios falsos.

Ciega, por un túnel de oro,
de espejos malos,
con la muerte
darás en un subterráneo.

Tú allí sola, con la muerte,
en un subterráneo.

Y alguien detrás, a tu espalda,
siempre.

DECEPTION

Someone behind you, right behind you,
covering your eyes with words.

Behind you, without a body,
without a soul.
Smoky voice of a dream
cut short.
Smoky voice
cut short.

With words, counterfeit glass.

Blindly, down a golden tunnel
of deceitful mirrors
you'll bump into death
somewhere underground.

You there all alone with death,
underground.

And someone behind you, right behind you,
always.

EL ÁNGEL ENVIDIOSO

Leñadoras son, ¡defiéndete!,
esas silbadoras hachas
que mueven mi lengua.

Hoces de los vientos malos,
¡alerta!,
que muerden mi alma.

Torre de desconfianza,
tú.
Tú, torre del oro, avara.
Ciega las ventanas.

O no, mira.

Hombres arrasados, fijos,
por las ciudades taladas.
Pregúntales.

O no, escucha.

Un cielo, verde de envidia,
rebosa mi boca y canta.

Yo, un cielo...

Ni escuches ni mires. Yo...
Ciega las ventanas.

THE ENVIOUS ANGEL

Defend yourself! They're woodcutters,
those whistling axes
moving my tongue.

Watch out!
Sickles of evil winds
biting my soul.

You,
tower of distrust.
You, tower of gold, greed.
Wall up your windows.

Better yet, look.

Men devastated, still,
in the fallen cities.
Ask them.

Better yet, listen.

A sky, green with envy,
overflows from my mouth and sings.

I, a sky . . .

Neither look nor listen. I . . .
Wall up your windows.

EL ÁNGEL TONTO

Ese ángel,
ese que niega el limbo de su fotografía
y hace pájaro muerto
su mano.

Ese ángel que teme que le pidan las alas,
que le besen el pico,
seriamente,
sin contrato.

Si es del cielo y tan tonto,
¿por qué en la tierra? Dime.
Decidme.

No en las calles, en todo,
indiferente, necio,
me lo encuentro.

¡El ángel tonto!

¡Si será de la tierra!
—Sí, de la tierra sólo.

THE STUPID ANGEL

That angel,
that one who refuses the limbo of his photograph
and makes a dead bird
of his hand.

That angel who's afraid they'll ask him for his wings,
and kiss him on the beak,
in all sincerity,
with no strings attached.

If he's from heaven and so stupid,
why is he on earth? Tell me.
Someone tell me.

I run into him,
indifferent, foolish,
not on the streets, but everywhere.

The stupid angel!

What if he's from earth!
"He is, from nowhere but earth."

EL ÁNGEL DEL MISTERIO

Un sueño sin faroles y una humedad de olvidos,
pisados por un nombre y una sombra.
No sé si por un nombre o muchos nombres,
si por una sombra o muchas sombras.
Reveládmelo.

Sé que habitan los pozos frías voces,
que son de un solo cuerpo o muchos cuerpos,
de un alma sola o muchas almas.
No sé.
Decídmelo.

Que un caballo sin nadie va estampando
a su amazona antigua por los muros.
Que en las almenas grita, muerto, alguien
que yo toqué, dormido, en un espejo,
que yo, mudo, le dije...
No sé.
Explicádmelo.

THE ANGEL OF MYSTERY

A dream unlit and a dampness of forgotten things
stepped on by a name and a shadow.
I don't know if by one name or many names,
one shadow or many shadows.
You tell me.

I know that cold voices live in wells,
that they belong to one body or many bodies,
one soul or many souls.
No I don't.
You decide.

That a riderless horse is stamping the image
of his ancient amazon upon the ramparts.
That on the battlements a corpse cries out,
someone I touched, asleep, in a mirror,
that I, speechless, spoke to . . .
I don't understand.
You explain it.

EL ÁNGEL BUENO

Vino el que yo quería,
el que yo llamaba.

No aquel que barre cielos sin defensas,
luceros sin cabañas,
lunas sin patria,
nieves.
Nieves de esas caídas de una mano,
un nombre,
un sueño,
una frente.

No aquel que a sus cabellos
ató la muerte.

El que yo quería.

Sin arañar los aires,
sin herir hojas ni mover cristales.

Aquel que a sus cabellos
ató el silencio.

Para, sin lastimarme,
cavar una ribera de luz dulce en mi pecho
y hacerme el alma navegable.

THE GOOD ANGEL

There came the one I wanted,
the one I called for.

Not the one that sweeps aside defenseless skies,
morning stars without huts,
moons without a country,
snows.
Snows of those who fell from a hand,
a name,
a dream,
a brow.

Not the one that tied death
to his hair.

The one I wanted.

Without scraping the air,
grazing a leaf or rattling a window.

The one that fastened silence
to his hair.

Came, to dig without pain
a shore of sweet light in my breast
and make my soul a sea.

EL ÁNGEL AVARO

Gentes de las esquinas
de pueblos y naciones que no están en el mapa,
comentaban.

Ese hombre está muerto
y no lo sabe.
Quiere asaltar la banca,
robar nubes, estrellas, cometas de oro,
comprar lo más difícil:
el cielo.
Y ese hombre está muerto.

Temblores subterráneos le sacuden la frente.
Tumbos de tierra desprendida,
ecos desvariados,
sones confusos de piquetas y azadas,
los oídos.
Los ojos,
luces de acetileno,
húmedas, áureas galerías.
El corazón,
explosiones de piedras, júbilos, dinamita.

Sueña con las minas.

THE GREEDY ANGEL

Crowds on streetcorners
of uncharted towns and countries,
were buzzing.

That man is dead
but doesn't know it.
He wants to rob the bank,
make off with clouds, stars, gold comets,
to buy what's dearest:
the sky.
And that man is dead.

Earthquakes shake his brow.
Landslides
crazed echoes,
muddled sounds of picks and shovels,
his ears.
His eyes,
acetylene torches,
wet, golden shafts.
His heart,
rock blasts, bursts of joy, dynamite.

He dreams of mines.

TRES RECUERDOS DEL CIELO

Homenaje a Gustavo Adolfo Bécquer.

PRÓLOGO

No habían cumplido años ni la rosa ni el arcángel.
Todo, anterior al balido y al llanto.
Cuando la luz ignoraba todavía
si el mar nacería niño o niña.
Cuando el viento soñaba melenas que peinar
y claveles el fuego que encender y mejillas
y el agua unos labios parados donde beber.
Todo, anterior al cuerpo, al nombre y al tiempo.

Entonces, yo recuerdo que, una vez, en el cielo...

PRIMER RECUERDO

> *... una azucena tronchada...*
> G. A. BÉCQUER.

Paseaba con un dejo de azucena que piensa,
casi de pájaro que sabe ha de nacer.
Mirándose sin verse a una luna que le hacía espejo el sueño
y a un silencio de nieve, que le elevaba los pies.
A un silencio asomada.
Era anterior al arpa, a la lluvia y a las palabras.
No sabía.
Blanca alumna del aire,
temblada con las estrellas, con la flor y los árboles.
Su tallo, su verde talle.
Con las estrellas mías
que, ignorantes de todo,
por cavar dos lagunas en sus ojos
la ahogaron en dos mares.

Y recuerdo...

Nada más: muerta, alejarse.

THREE MEMORIES OF HEAVEN

Homage to Gustavo Adolfo Bécquer

PROLOGUE

The rose and the archangel had not been born.
It was the time before the bleating and tears
when light still did not know
if the sea would be male or female,
when wind dreamed of long hair to comb
and fire dreamed of cheeks and carnations to burn
and water of lips stopping to drink.
It was before the body, before name and time.

It was then, I remember, that once long ago, in heaven . . .

FIRST MEMORY

> *. . . a lily cut down . . .*
> G. A. BÉCQUER

She walked with the abandon of a brooding lily,
almost like a bird that knows it will be born.
She looked but could not see herself in that moon
     her dream had made into a mirror
and into a silence of snow, that lifted her feet.
She gazed into silence.
It was the time before the harp, before rain and words.
She didn't know.
White school girl of the air,
she trembled with the stars, with the flower and trees.
And her stem, her green shape
trembled with my stars who,
ignorant of everything,
tried to carve out inlets in her eyes
only to drown her in those two seas.

I remember . . .

Nothing more: she was dead, going away.

SEGUNDO RECUERDO

> *...rumor de besos y batir de alas...*
> G. A. BÉCQUER.

También antes,
mucho antes de la rebelión de las sombras,
de que al mundo cayeran plumas incendiadas
y un pájaro pudiera ser muerto por un lirio.
Antes, antes que tú me preguntaras
el número y el sitio de mi cuerpo.
Mucho antes del cuerpo.
En la época del alma.
Cuando tú abriste en la frente sin corona, del cielo,
la primera dinastía del sueño.
Cuando tú, al mirarme en la nada,
inventaste la primera palabra.

Entonces, nuestro encuentro.

TERCER RECUERDO

> *...detrás del abanico*
> *de plumas de oro...*
> G. A. BÉCQUER.

Aún los valses del cielo no habían desposado al jazmín y la nieve,
ni los aires pensado en la posible música de tus cabellos,
ni decretado el rey que la violeta se enterrara en un libro.
No.
Era la era en que la golondrina viajaba
sin nuestras iniciales en el pico.
En que las campanillas y las enredaderas
morían sin balcones que escalar y estrellas.
La era
en que al hombro de un ave no había flor que apoyara la cabeza.

Entonces, detrás de tu abanico, nuestra luna primera.

SECOND MEMORY

. . . a murmur of kisses and of beating wings . . .
G. A. BÉCQUER

It was also before,
long before the rebellion of shadows,
long before burning feathers fell into the world
and a bird could be killed by a lily.
It was even before you could ask me
the number and place of my body.
It was long before the body.
It was in the time of the soul
when you opened in the uncrowned brow of heaven
the first dynasty of dreams,
when you looked at me in nothingness
and invented the first word.

It was then we first met.

THIRD MEMORY

. . . behind that fan
of golden feathers . . .
G. A. BÉCQUER

Heaven's waltzes had not yet wed jasmine to the snow,
nor air dreamt of that possible music in your hair,
nor the king decreed the violet be buried in a book.
No.
It was the time when the swallow traveled
without our initials in her beak,
when bellflowers and bindweed
died without balconies to climb, without stars.
It was the time
when no flower leaned its head on the shoulder of a bird.

It was then, behind your fan, we saw our first moon.

EL ÁNGEL DE ARENA

Seriamente, en tus ojos era la mar dos niños que me espiaban,
temerosos de lazos y palabras duras.
Dos niños de la noche, terribles, expulsados del cielo,
cuya infancia era un robo de barcos y un crimen de soles y de lunas.
Duérmete. Ciérralos.

Vi que el mar verdadero era un muchacho que saltaba desnudo,
invitándome a un plato de estrellas y a un reposo de algas.
¡Sí, sí! Ya mi vida iba a ser, ya lo era, litoral desprendido.
Pero tú, despertando, me hundiste en tus ojos.

THE ANGEL OF SAND

I mean it, in your eyes the sea was two children watching me,
afraid of traps and stern words.
Two dreadful children of the night, expelled from heaven,
their childhood a theft of boats and a crime of suns and moons.
Go to sleep. Close your eyes.

I saw the true sea was a naked boy, skipping,
offering me a dish of stars and a nap of seaweed.
Yes, yes! Now my life would be, in fact was, a generous shore.
But you woke up and drowned me in your eyes.

EL MAL MINUTO

Cuando para mí eran los trigos viviendas de astros y de dioses
y la escarcha los lloros helados de una gacela,
alguien me enyesó el pecho y la sombra,
traicionándome.

Ese minuto fue el de las balas perdidas,
el del secuestro, por el mar, de los hombres que quisieron ser pájaros,
el del telegrama a deshora y el hallazgo de sangre,
el de la muerte del agua que siempre miró al cielo.

THE EVIL MOMENT

When wheat was for me the home of stars and gods
and frost the frozen tears of a gazelle,
someone set my breast and shadow in plaster,
and betrayed me.

At that moment bullets went wild,
the sea kidnapped men who wanted to be birds,
the telegram came at the wrong time and blood was discovered,
and water that always looked to heaven died.

EL ÁNGEL DE LAS BODEGAS

1

Fue cuando la flor del vino se moría en penumbra
y dijeron que el mar la salvaría del sueño.
Aquel día bajé a tientas a tu alma encalada y húmeda.
Y comprobé que un alma oculta frío y escaleras
y que más de una ventana puede abrir con su eco otra voz,
    si es buena.

Te vi flotar a ti, flor de agonía, flotar sobre tu mismo espíritu.
(Alguien había jurado que el mar te salvaría del sueño.)
Fue cuando comprobé que murallas se quiebran con suspiros
y que hay puertas al mar que se abren con palabras.

2

La flor del vino, muerta en los toneles,
sin haber visto nunca la mar, la nieve.

La flor del vino, sin probar el té,
sin haber visto nunca un piano de cola.

Cuatro arrumbadores encalan los barriles.
Los vinos dulces, llorando, se embarcan a deshora.

La flor del vino blanco, sin haber visto el mar, muerta.
Las penumbras se beben el aceite y un ángel la cera.

He aquí paso a paso toda mi larga historia.
Guardadme el secreto, aceitunas, abejas.

THE ANGEL OF THE WINE CELLARS

1

It was when the flower of the wine was dying in half-darkness
and they said the sea would save it from sleep.
On that day, I stumbled down into your damp and
     whitewashed soul
and learned that the soul hides cold and stairs
and that another voice can open with its echo more than one
     window, if it's good.

I saw you floating there, flower of agony, floating on your
     own spirit.
(Someone had sworn the sea would save you from sleep.)
It was when I learned for sure that walls are broken with sighs
and there are doors to the sea which are opened with words.

2

The flower of the wine, dead in the barrels,
without ever having seen the sea, the snow.

The flower of the wine, never having tasted tea,
without ever having seen a grand piano.

Four coopers coat the barrels with water and lime.
The sweet wines, in tears, are shipped before their time.

The flower of the white wine, without ever having seen the
     sea, dead.
The half-darkness drinks up the oil and an angel the wax.

Here, step by step, is my whole, long history.
Keep my secret, olives, honeybees.

LOS ÁNGELES COLEGIALES

Ninguno comprendíamos el secreto nocturno de las pizarras
ni por qué la esfera armilar se exaltaba tan sola cuando la mirábamos.
Sólo sabíamos que una circunferencia puede no ser redonda
y que un eclipse de luna equivoca a las flores
y adelanta el reloj de los pájaros.

Ninguno comprendíamos nada:
ni por qué nuestros dedos eran de tinta china
y la tarde cerraba compases para al alba abrir libros.
Sólo sabíamos que una recta, si quiere, puede ser curva o quebrada
y que las estrellas errantes son niños que ignoran la aritmética.

THE GRADE SCHOOL ANGELS

None of us understood the night secret of these blackboards
nor why the armillary sphere got so excited only when
    we looked at it.
We knew only that a circumference might not be round
and that an eclipse of the moon confuses flowers
and makes the inner clock of birds go faster.

None of us understood anything:
not even why our fingers were made of India ink
or why dusk closed compasses to open books at dawn.
We knew only that a straight line, if it wants, can be
    curved or broken
and that the wandering stars are children who don't
    know arithmetic.

NIEVE VIVA

Sin mentir, ¡qué mentira de nieve anduvo muda por mi sueño!
Nieve sin voz, quizás de ojos azules, lenta y con cabellos.
¿Cuándo la nieve al mirar distraída movió bucles de fuego?
Anduvo muda blanqueando las preguntas que no se respondieron,
los olvidados y borrados sepulcros para estrenar nuevos recuerdos.
Dando a cenizas, ya en el aire, forma de luz sin hueso.

SNOW ALIVE

In truth, what a lie of snow walked silently through my dream!
Voiceless snow, slow, with blue eyes perhaps, and hair.
When did the snow with a casual glance move curls of fire?
It walked without a word, whitening the unanswered questions,
the forgotten and crossed-out graves, to introduce new memories.
Shaping ashes, already in the air, into boneless light.

EL ÁNGEL SUPERVIVIENTE

Acordaos.
La nieve traía gotas de lacre, de plomo derretido
y disimulos de niña que ha dado muerte a un cisne.
Una mano enguantada, la dispersión de la luz y el lento
      asesinato.
La derrota del cielo, un amigo.

Acordaos de aquel día, acordaos
y no olvidéis qua la sorpresa paralizó el pulso y el color
      de los astros.
En el frío, murieron dos fantasmas.
Por un ave, tres anillos de oro
fueron hallados y enterrados en la escarcha.
La última voz de un hombre ensangrentó el viento.
Todos los ángeles perdieron la vida.
Menos uno, herido, alicortado.

THE SURVIVING ANGEL

Remember.
The snow brought drops of sealing wax, of molten lead
and the coy looks of a little girl who's killed a swan.
A gloved hand, the scattering of light and the slow murder.
The rout of the sky, a friend.

Remember that day, remember it
and don't forget that surprise paralyzed the pulse and color
    of the stars.
In the cold two phantoms died.
A bird found three golden rings
and buried them in the frost.
A man's last voice stained the wind with blood.
All the angels lost their lives.
Except one, wounded, whose wings were clipped.

SERMONES Y MORADAS

[1929~1930]

SERMONS AND DWELLINGS

SIN MÁS REMEDIO

Tenía yo que salir de la tierra,
la tierra tenía que escupirme de una vez para siempre
      como un hijo bastardo,
come un hijo temido a quien no esperan nunca reconocer
      las ciudades.
Había que llorar hasta mover los trenes y trastornar a
      gritos las horas de las mareas,
dando al cielo motivo para abandonarse a una pena sin
      lluvia.
Había que expatriarse involuntariamente,
dejar ciertas alcobas,
ciertos ecos,
ciertos ojos vacíos.

Ya voy.

Tenías tú que vivir más de una media vida sin conocer
      las voces que ya llegan pasadas por el mundo,
más aislado que el frío de una torre encargada de iluminar
      el rumbo de las aves perdidas,
sobre el mar que te influye hasta hacerte saladas las
      palabras.
Tú tenías a la fuerza que haber nacido solo y sufrido sin
      gloria para decirme:

Hace ya treinta años que ni leo los periódicos: mañana
      hará buen tiempo.

WITHOUT A DOUBT

I had to leave this earth
and the earth had to spit me out once and for all
        like some bastard son,
like a feared son the cities never hope to claim as
        their own.
We had to weep until the trains moved and our shouts
        disrupted the timetable of the tides,
giving the sky an excuse to wallow in a rainless sorrow.
We had to go into involuntary exile,
leave certain bedrooms,
certain echoes,
certain empty eyes.

I'm leaving now.

You had to have lived more than half a life not recognizing
        the already faded voices in this world,
more isolated than the cold of a tower
        charged with lighting the way of lost birds,
and lived about the sea that affected you to the
        point it made your words salty.
You surely would have had to have been born alone
        and suffered ingloriously to tell me:

I stopped reading newspapers thirty years ago:
        the weather will be fine tomorrow.

YO ANDUVE TODA UNA NOCHE CON
LOS OJOS CERRADOS

Se moría la vía láctea por dormir una hora tan sólo sobre
    los trigos,
una hora siquiera para olvidar tanto camino derramado,
tanto último eco de almas anónimas de héroes recuperadas
    por el aire.
Ya sé salvarme a ciegas de esas torres que han de preguntar
    al alba por el origen de mi cuna.
Soy ése,
ese mismo que sigue la ruta aérea de su sangre sin querer
    abrir los ojos.
Nacen pájaros que corren el peligro de estrellarse contra
    los astros más próximos.

Mis pies han demostrado que si hay piedras en el cielo
    son casi inofensivas
allí donde las manos escogen para reposo la penumbra de
    las guitarras
y los cabellos recuerdan todavía el llanto de los sauces
    cuando fallecen los ríos.
Mañana me oiréis afirmar que aún existen alturas donde
    los oídos perciben el rastro de una hoja muerta diez
    siglos antes y ese nombre velado que flota en el
    descenso de las voces desaparecidas.
Ya a mí no me hace falta para nada comprobar la
    redondez de la Tierra.

I WALKED ONE WHOLE NIGHT WITH
MY EYES CLOSED

The Milky Way was dying to lie down for just one
    hour on the wheat,
one hour to forget so much spilled road,
so many last echoes of heroic, anonymous souls
    retrieved by the wind.
I know now how to escape blindly those towers that will
    question the dawn about the origin of my birth.
I am he,
he who follows the airways of his blood without
    wanting to open his eyes.
Some birds are born to risk being smashed against
    the nearest stars.

My feet have proved that if there are stones in the
    sky they are virtually harmless
there where hands choose to rest in the shadow
    of guitars
and hair still recalls the weeping of willows
    when rivers die.
Tomorrow, you will hear me proclaim that there are heights
    where the ear hears the trail of a leaf
        dead ten centuries and that muffled name
        floating in the descent of vanished voices.
I no longer need to prove the Earth is round.

ADIÓS A LA SANGRE

Yo me decía adiós llorando en los andenes.
Sujetadme,
sujetad a mi sangre,
paredes,
muros que la veláis y que la separáis de otras sangres que
    duermen.
¿Yo me decía adiós porque iba hacia la muerte?

Ahora,
cuando yo diga *ahora,*
haced que el fuego y los astros que iban a caer se hielen.
Que yo no diga nunca esa palabra en los trenes.

Porque,
escuchad:
¿es vuestra sangre la que grita al hundirse en el agua con
    los puentes?

GOODBYE TO BLOOD

I would tell myself goodbye as I wept on the platforms.
Hold me,
hold back my blood,
you walls,
you ramparts that watch over it and separate it from
     sleeping blood.
Was I telling myself goodbye because I was heading
     toward death?

Now,
when I say *now,*
make the fire and stars about to fall freeze.
So that I never say that word on trains.

Because,
listen:
Is it your blood that is groaning as it sinks into the
     water with those bridges?

FRAGMENTOS DE UN DESEO

... Aquí, cuando el aire traiciona la rectitud de los lirios,
es condenado a muerte por un remolino de agua.
No es sombra de amargura la que adelantan los árboles
        hacia el ocaso.
Te informará de esto el guardabosque que costean los fríos.

Si en tu país una ilusión se pierde a lo largo de los calores,
en el mío las nieves te ayudarán a encontrarla.
Si la huella de un zapato no dispone de tiempo para dormir
        a una violeta,
aquí entretiene su vida en recoger el ciclo de las lluvias.

Es triste,
muy triste saber que una mano estampada en el polvo
dura menos que el recorrido que abre una hoja al morirse.

¿No te apenan esos hilos que desfallecen de pronto contra
        tus mejillas
cuando despobladas de nubes se hielan en los estanques?

FRAGMENTS OF A WISH

Here, when air betrays the rectitude of lilies,
it is condemned to death by a whirlpool of water.
It is not the shadow of bitterness these trees
    cast toward the sunset.
The forester whom the cold pays will tell you this.

If in your country in the heat of the summer
    you lose your dream
the snows of mine will help you find it.
If the footprint of a shoe has no time to put a
    violet to sleep,
here it can pass the time charting the cycles of rain.

It is sad,
very sad to know that a hand stamped into the dust
lasts less time than the path a leaf opens when it dies.

Don't you grieve for those threads that suddenly
    die against your cheeks
when, emptied of clouds, they freeze in pools?

ELEGÍAS

1.—La pena de los jarros sin agua caídos en el destierro de los objetos difuntos.

2.—La noticia del crimen de la noche, abandonada entre cardos, muelles rotos y latones viejos.

3.—La botella que no se rompió al caer y vive con el gollete clavado en los oasis de las basuras.

4.—La venda rota de una herida, arrastrada por las hormigas de las tres de la tarde.

5.—Esos chorros de agua de carbón que desvelan el sueño boquiabierto de los túneles.

6.—El moscón que se clava de cabeza en la espina de un cardo.

7.—La caja vacía de cerillas junto al excremento de los caballos.

ELEGIES

1.—The grief of empty pitchers fallen into the exile of dead objects.
2.—The news of the crime in the night, abandoned among thistles, broken springs and old cans.
3.—The bottle that didn't break when it fell and lives with its neck stuck in the oasis of rubbish.
4.—The ragged bandage of a wound, dragged along by ants at three in the afternoon.
5.—Those streams of black water that keep awake the gaping sleep of tunnels.
6.—The blowfly that dives headfirst into the thorn of a thistle.
7.—The empty box of matches near horse manure.

ENTRE EL CLAVEL Y LA ESPADA

[1939-1940]

BETWEEN THE CARNATION AND THE SWORD

3

METAMORFOSIS DEL CLAVEL

METAMORPHOSIS OF
THE CARNATION

1

Junto a la mar y un río y en mis primeros años,
quería ser caballo.

Las orillas de juncos eran de viento y yeguas.
Quería ser caballo.

Las colas empinadas barrían las estrellas.
Quería ser caballo.

Escucha por la playa, madre, mi trote largo.
Quería ser caballo.

Desde mañana, madre, viviré junto al agua.
Quería ser caballo.

En el fondo dormía una niña cuatralba.
Quería ser caballo.

1

By the sea and a river and in my early days,
I wanted to be a horse.

The shores of rushes were made of wind and mares.
I wanted to be a horse.

Their lofty tails brushed the stars.
I wanted to be a horse.

Mother, listen to my long stride on the beach.
I wanted to be a horse.

Mother, from tomorrow on, I will live by the water.
I wanted to be a horse.

At the bottom of the sea slept a four-legged girl.
I wanted to be a horse.

3

Un clavel va de viaje,
un clavel va viajando:
por las piernas, mar arriba,
por los pechos, mar abajo.

Un clavel va de viaje,
un clavel ya ha naufragado.

¿Qué será, qué no será,
que era rojo y ahora es blanco?

3

A carnation goes on a journey,
a carnation is journeying:
its legs take it upstream,
its breasts, downstream.

A carnation goes on a journey,
a carnation already shipwrecked.

What can it be? What can't it be?
Something that was red and now is white?

4

Me fui.
Las conchas están cerradas.
Aquel ciego olor a espuma
siempre se acordó de mí.

Siempre me buscaba.

Me fui.
Estoy torciendo limones
a un plato de agua salada.
Siempre me acordé de ti.

Siempre te encontraba.

Me fui.
Las conchas siguen cerradas.

4

I left.
The shells are closed.
That blind odor of foam
remembered me always.

It looked for me always.

I left.
I am squeezing lemons
into a plate of salt water.
I remembered you always.

I found you always.

I left.
The shells are still closed.

5

¿Qué tengo en la mano?
(¡Que se te convierte en concha!)

¿Qué tengo en la mano?
(¡Que se te convierte en árbol!)

¿Qué tengo en la mano?
(¡Que se te convierte en hojas!)

¿Qué tengo en la mano?
(¡Que se te convierte en nardos!)

5

What do I have in my hand?
(Watch it turn into a shell!)

What do I have in my hand?
(Watch it turn into a tree!)

What do I have in my hand?
(Watch it turn into leaves!)

What do I have in my hand?
(Watch it turn into spikenards!)

6

(A Ninoche)

El caballo pidió sábanas,
rizadas como los ríos.
Sábanas blancas.

Quiero ser hombre una noche.
Llamadme al alba.

La mujer no lo llamó.
(Nunca más volvió a su cuadra.)

6

(To Ninoche)

The horse asked for sheets,
sheets that rippled like rivers.
White ones.

For just one night I want to be a man.
Call me at dawn.

The woman didn't call him.
(He never went back to his stable.)

7

Las fuentes eran de vino.
Los mares, de uvas moradas.

Pedías agua.

Bajó el calor al arroyo.
El arroyo era de mosto.

Pedías agua.

Tiritaba el toro. El fuego
era de moscatel negro.

Pedías agua.

(Dos ramos de vino dulce
te saltaron de los pechos.)

7

The springs were wine.
The seas, purple grapes.

You begged for water.

The heat sank into the arroyo.
The arroyo was of must.

You begged for water.

The bull was shivering. The fire
was black muscatel.

You begged for water.

(Two streams of sweet wine
spurted from your breasts.)

8

Se equivocó la paloma.
Se equivocaba.

Por ir al norte, fue al sur.
Creyó que el trigo era agua.
Se equivocaba.

Creyó que el mar era el cielo;
que la noche, la mañana.
Se equivocaba.

Que las estrellas, rocío;
que la calor, la nevada.
Se equivocaba.

Que tu falda era tu blusa;
que tu corazón, su casa.
Se equivocaba.

(Ella se durmió en la orilla.
Tú, en la cumbre de una rama.)

8

The dove made a mistake.
It was mistaken.

To go North, it went South.
It thought that wheat was water.
It was mistaken.

It thought the sea was the sky;
that night was morning.
It was mistaken.

That stars were dew;
that heat was fallen snow.
It was mistaken.

That your skirt was your blouse;
that your heart was its home.
It was mistaken.

(It slept on the shore.
And you, on top of a bough.)

10

Mamaba el toro, mamaba
la leche de la serrana.

Al toro se le ponían
ojos de muchacha.

Ya que eres toro, mi hijo,
dame una cornada.

Verás que tengo otro toro
entre las entrañas.

(La madre se volvió yerba,
y el toro, toro de agua.)

10

The bull was sucking, sucking
the milk of the mountain woman.

His eyes turned into
the eyes of a young woman.

Since you are a bull, my son,
gore me.

You will find that I have another bull
in my guts.

(The mother turned into grass,
and the bull, into a bull of water.)

12

Se despertó una mañana.
Soy la yerba.
llena de agua.

Me llamo yerba. Si crezco,
puedo llamarme cabello.

Me llamo yerba. Si salto,
puedo ser rumor de árbol.

Si grito, puedo ser pájaro.
Si vuelo...

(Hubo temblores de yerba
aquella noche en el cielo.)

12

It awoke one morning.
I am grass,
full of water.

My name is grass. If I grow,
I can call myself hair.

My name is grass. If I spring up,
I can become the whisper of a tree.

If I call out, I can become a bird.
If I fly . . .

(There were grassquakes
that night in the sky.)

13

¡Amor!, gritó el loro.
(Nadie le contestó de un chopo a otro.)

¡Amor, amor mío!
(Silencio de pino a pino.)

¡Amooor!
(Tampoco el río le oyó.)

¡Me muero!

(Ni el chopo,
ni el pino,
ni el río
fueron a su entierro.)

13

Love! screeched the parrot.
(No one answered from the poplars.)

My love, my love!
(Silence in the pines.)

Looove!
The river didn't hear it either.

I'm dying!

(Neither the poplar,
or the pine,
or the river,
went to its funeral.)

14

Cierra la llave de paso.
Se calló el agua.
(Pero en lo oscuro seguía sonando.)

¿En dónde está, que la yerba
se muere ahogada?
(Seguía sonando.)

La mula se sintió madre.
Dio a luz el alba.
(No sonaba.)

14

You turn off the faucet.
The water stopped running.
(But in the dark it kept on running.)

And since the grass is drowning
where is the water?
(It kept on running.)

The mule became pregnant.
Dawn gave birth.
(The water stopped.)

16

Tunas y pitas gritaron,
feroces de ansiosas púas
las manos.

El viento
quiso desenmarañar
sus arrancados cabellos.

Le arañaron. No quisieron.

La aurora
la encontró muerta en la noria.

Sendas de sangre le hallaron
en los nacientes del pecho.

(Amalia, catorce años.)

16

Prickly pears and agaves cried out,
their hands
raging with anxious thorns.

The wind wanted to untangle
its torn-out hair.

They scratched it. They didn't mean to.

Dawn
found her dead in the waterwheel.

They found traces of blood
in the budding breasts.

(Amalia, 14 years old.)

18

El perro lobo llamó
a la puerta de la casa.

Insomnio turbio en la alcoba.
Una muchacha.

Tengo amor de hombre y tengo
de hombre también la palabra.

Alba.

Entre los rastros del monte
se vieron huellas humanas.

Consuelo dulce el clavel.
GÓNGORA.

18

The wolfhound called
at the door of the house.

Restless insomnia in the bedroom.
A young woman.

I feel a man's love and I have
a man's word besides.

Dawn.

Among the tracks on the mountain
human footprints were seen.

Sweet comfort the carnation
GÓNGORA

4

TORO EN EL MAR
(ELEGÍA SOBRE UN MAPA PERDIDO)

BULL IN THE SEA
(ELEGY FOR A LOST MAP)

1

A aquel país se lo venían diciendo
desde hace tanto tiempo.
Mírate y lo verás.
Tienes forma de toro,
de piel de toro abierto,
tendido sobre el mar.

(De verde toro muerto.)

1

They had been saying it to that country
for such a long time.
Look at yourself and you will see it.
You have the shape of a bull,
the skin of a bull torn open,
stretched out upon the sea.

(Of a green bull dead.)

2

Mira, en aquel país
ahora se puede navegar en sangre.
Un soplo de silencio y de vacío
puede de norte a sur, y sin dejar la tierra,
llevarte.

2

Look, in that country
you can now sail on blood.
A gust of silence and emptiness
can transport you from North to South, and
without leaving land.

3

Eras jardín de naranjas.
Huerta de mares abiertos.
Tiemblo de olivas de pámpanos,
los verdes cuernos.

Con pólvora te regaron.
Y fuiste toro de fuego.

3

You were a garden of orange trees.
An orchard of open seas.
A stirring of olive trees and vines,
those green horns.

They sprayed you with gunpowder.
And you became a bull of fire.

4

Le están dando a este toro
pastos amargos,
yerbas con sustancia de muertos,
negras hieles
y clara sangre ingenua de soldado.
¡Ay, qué mala comida para este toro verde,
acostumbrado a las libres dehesas y a los ríos,
para este toro a quien la mar y el cielo
eran aún pequeños como establo!

4

They are grazing this bull
in bitter pastures,
on grass with the substance of dead bodies,
black bile
and clear, guileless soldiers' blood.
What bad food for this green bull,
accustomed to the open range and rivers,
for this bull for whom the sea and the sky
were small as a stable!

5

Sobre un campo de anémonas,
cayó muerto el soldado.
Las anémonas blancas,
de grana lo lloraron.
De los montes vinieron jabalíes
y un río se llenó de muslos blancos.

5

In a field of anemones
the soldier fell.
The white anemones
wore his red in grief.
From the mountains came wild boars
and a river filled with white thighs.

6

No se podía dormir, porque escuchaba
abrirse hoyos y hoyos en la tierra.
No se podía andar, no se podía.
Los pasos ya no eran,
ya no eran pasos, porque todo el cuerpo
era lo que se hundía,
lo que había de hundirse ...
                              ... y se iba hundiendo.

6

He couldn't sleep, because he was listening
to hole after hole opening in the earth.
You couldn't walk, you just couldn't.
There were no longer footsteps,
no longer footsteps, because the whole body
was what was sinking,
what had to be sinking . . .

                                    . . . and was sinking.

7

Habría que llorar.
Sólo ortigas y cardos,
y un triste barro frío,
ya siempre, en los zapatos.

Cuando murió el soldado,
lejos, escaló el mar una ventana
y se puso a llorar junto a un retrato.

Habría que contarlo.

7

You had to weep.
Nothing but nettles and thistles
and a dismal mud forever
frozen to his shoes.

When the soldier died,
far off, the sea stole through a window
and began to weep beside a portrait.

You had to tell it.

8

Todo oscuro, terrible. Aquella luna
que se rompió, de pronto, echando sangre.
Aquel desprevenido silencio
que de pronto impedía que mojase
la sangre al corazón, abriendo puertas
para dejarlo hundido, abandonado,
dentro de un uniforme
sin nadie.

Todo oscuro, terrible.

Mas cuando fue a entender lo que quería,
ya tan sólo era un traje.

8

Everything was dark, appalling. That moon
which shattered suddenly, spurting blood.
That unprepared silence
which suddenly blocked the blood
from soaking the heart, opening doors
leaving it in ruins, abandoned,
inside a uniform
without anybody.

Everything was dark, appalling.

But just as he was about to find out what he wanted,
he was nothing but a suit.

9

... Y le daré, si vuelvo, una toronja
y una jarra de barro vidriado,
de esas que se parecen a sus pechos
cuando saltan de un árbol a otro árbol.

Pero en vez del soldado,
sólo llegó una voz despavorida
que encaneció el recuerdo de los álamos.

9

. . . And I'll give her, if I return, a grapefruit
and a glazed earthenware jar,
one that looks just like her breasts
when they swing from one tree to another.

But instead of the soldier,
there came only a terrified cry
that turned the memory of the poplars gray.

10

Sonaba el miedo a gozne sin aceite,
a inviolado jardín y a tabla seca.
Olía a viento de pasillo oscuro
y a invisible mantel
goteado de cera.

(Cuando salió el soldado de la celda,
sobre la tapia izó el fusil al cielo,
ondeando una toca por bandera.)

10

Fear like the sound of an unoiled hinge,
a cloistered garden and dry wood.
Like the smell in a dark passageway,
and an invisible altar cloth
spotted with wax.

(When the soldier came out of the cell,
he raised his rifle over the wall
pointing to heaven,
waving a nun's headdress for a flag.)

11

¡Ay, a este verde toro
le están achicharrando, ay, la sangre!
Todos me lo han cogido de los cuernos
y que quieras que no me lo han volcado
por tierra, pateándolo,
extendiéndolo a golpes de metales candentes,
sobre la mar hirviendo.
Verde toro inflamado, ¡ay, ay!,
que llenas de lamentos e iluminas, helándola,
esta desventurada noche
donde se mueven sombras ya verdaderamente sombras,
o ya desencajadas sombras vivas
que las han de tapar también las piedras.

¡Ay verde toro, ay,
que eras toro de trigo,
toro de lluvia y sol, de cierzo y nieve,
triste hoguera atizada hoy en medio del mar,
del mar, del mar ardiendo!

11

They are burning to a crisp the blood
of this green bull!
Everyone's got him by the horns
and, like it or not, have slammed him
to the ground, kicking him,
hammering him flat with red hot irons,
upon the boiling sea.
Oh green bull on fire,
you who fill with cries, you who illuminate, freezing it,
this forsaken night
of moving shadows, of true shadows,
or of dissolving shadows
stones will also cover!

Oh green bull,
once a bull of wheat,
a bull of rain and sun, North wind and snow,
a sorrowful bonfire now in the middle of the sea,
the sea, in the middle of the burning sea!

12

La muerte estaba a mi lado,
la muerte estaba a tu lado.
La veía
y la veías.

Sonaba en todo la muerte,
llamaba a todo la muerte.
La sentía
y la sentías.

No quiso verme ni verte.

12

Death was at my side,
death was at your side.
I saw it
and you saw it.

Death echoed in everything,
death called for everything.
I heard it
and you heard it.

It was unwilling to see you or me.

13

Como aquellas que ardían, trasminando,
blancas, sobre los árboles abiertos,
e iguales para el hoyo de las manos.

(Cuando una bala le partió su sueño,
de entre la tierra que tapó al soldado
dos magnolias subieron,
dos magnolias iguales que tenían
por raíces sus dedos.)

13

Like those that were burning, blasting,
white, through the opened trees,
and a perfect fit for the hollow of hands.

(When a bullet burst his dream,
from the earth that covered the soldier
two magnolias rose,
two perfectly matched magnolias that had
his fingers for roots.)

14

La carta del soldado terminaba:
"Y hallará el alba, amor, en esa noche
más sitio en las orillas de las sábanas".
Pero el alba que vino
venía con un nudo en la garganta.

14

The soldier's letter ended:
"And on that night, my love, the dawn
will find more room on both shores of the sheets."
But the dawn that broke
brought a lump in its throat.

15

El soldado soñaba, aquel soldado
de tierra adentro, oscuro: —Si ganamos,
la llevaré a que mire los naranjos,
a que toque la mar, que nunca ha visto,
y se le llene el corazón de barcos.

Pero vino la paz. Y era un olivo
de interminable sangre por el campo.

15

The soldier, that dark soldier
from the interior, dreamed: "If we win,
I will bring her to see the orange trees,
to touch the sea she's never seen,
and feast her heart on sailing ships."

But peace came. And he was an olive tree
of blood flooding the fields.

17

Mas cuando ya a los años que se tienen
nos corren por la sangre ya más muertos que años,
lo mejor es ser álamo.
Álamo que ha asistido a una batalla
y va contando noches con nombres de soldados.

17

Now that we've reached the age
when more corpses than years run through our blood,
it is better to be a poplar.
A poplar that has seen a battle
and goes on counting nights with soldiers' names.

18

Aquel olor a inesperada muerte,
a soldado sin nombre y sin familia,
dando a los hormigueros de la tierra
quizás el mejor traje de su vida,
de la vera de un olmo
se me llevó el aroma de mi amiga.

18

That odor of unexpected death,
of a soldier nameless and without family,
surrendering to the ant hills of this earth
probably the best suit he ever owned,
on the fringe of an elm
snatched away my love's fragrance.

19

(Muelle del Reloj)

A través de una niebla caporal de tabaco
miro al río de Francia
moviendo escombros tristes, arrastrando ruinas
por el pesado verde ricino de sus aguas.
Mis ventanas
ya no dan a los álamos y los ríos de España.

Quiero mojar la mano en tan espeso frío
y parar lo que pasa
por entre ciegas bocas de piedra, dividiendo
subterráneas corrientes de muertos y cloacas.
Mis ventanas
ya no dan a los álamos y los ríos de España.

Miro una lenta piel de toro desollado,
sola, descuartizada,
sosteniendo cadáveres de voces conocidas,
sombra abajo, hacia el mar, hacia una mar sin barcas.
Mis ventanas,
ya no dan a los álamos y los ríos de España.

Desgraciada viajera fluvial que de mis ojos
desprendidos arrancas
eso que de sus cuencas desciende como río
cuando el llanto se olvida de rodar como lágrima.
Mis ventanas,
ya no dan a los álamos y los ríos de España.

19

(Clock Spring)

Through a fog of coarse tobacco
I look at this river of France
hauling dismal rubble, dragging debris
along the thick green castor oil of its waters.
My windows
look out no more on the poplars and rivers of Spain.

I want to soak my hand in so much of this thick cold
and stop what's flowing past
between blind stone mouths, separating
underground currents of corpses and sewage.
My windows
look out no more on the poplars and rivers of Spain.

I look at this bull's frail skin,
all alone, cut to shreds,
bearing bodies with familiar voices,
it's shadow heading down towards the sea, towards a boatless sea.
My windows
look out no more on the poplars and rivers of Spain.

Sad flowing traveler pulling
from my unhinged eyes
what pours from their sockets like rivers
when tears forget to turn into tears.
My windows
look out no more on the poplars and rivers of Spain.

20

Querías despertarte, pobre toro,
abrumada de nieblas la cabeza.
Querías sacudir la hincada cola
y el obligado párpado caído refrescarlo en el mar,
mojándote de verde las pupilas.
Resollabas de sangre, rebasado, abarcado,
oprimido de noche y de terrores,
bramando por abrir una brecha en el cielo
y sonrosarte un poco de dulce aurora
los despoblados ramos de tus astas.

Gaviotas amarillas
y despistados pájaros de tierra
tejían sobre ellas
silenciosas coronas de silbos tristes y alas.

Niños muertos perdidos rodaban los delfines
por tus desfallecidas riberas
de lagares y aceite derramados,
mientras que tú, alejándote,
dejabas en mis ojos el deseo
de alzarte de rodillas sobre el mar,
encendiendo otra vez sobre tu lomo
el sol, la luna, el viento y las estrellas.

(Estrecho de Gibraltar.)

20

You wanted to wake up, poor bull,
your head fogbound.
You wanted to swish your stiff tail
and cool your drooping eyelids in the sea,
greening the pupils.
Overcome by night and terror,
crushed, trapped, you
snorted blood, bellowing
to break open the sky
and dip in the blush of sweet dawn
the barren branches of your horns.

Yellow sea gulls
and land birds off course
wove on them
silent wreaths of sad bird calls and wings.

Dolphins rolled lost dead children
to your sinking shores
of oilspill and winepress refuse,
as you went away,
leaving my eyes desiring
to raise you, on your knees, above the sea,
the sun, the moon, the wind and the stars
once more lighting up your back.

(Strait of Gibraltar)

21

Canario solo en el mar.
Canta al toro que se aleja,
que se va.

Las gaviotas de los palos
ya no están.
La lluvia las mandó a tierra.

Canta al toro que se aleja.

En el mar perdí la mar
y en tierra perdí la tierra.

Que se va,
canta al toro que se va.

21

A canary alone at sea.
It sings to the bull which is going,
which is leaving.

The seagulls of the pilings
are no longer there.
The rain grounded them.

It sings to the bull which is going.

At sea I lost the sea
and on land I lost the land.

It sings,
It sings to the bull which is leaving.

22

Te oigo mugir en medio de la noche
por encima del mar, también bramando.
Y salgo a oírte, sin dominio, a tientas,
a ver entre la helada y el sonoro
crecimiento tranquilo de los pastos
cómo va descendiendo hasta mi inmóvil
desolación ese desierto tuyo,
ese arenal de muertos
que sopla de tu voz sobre las sombras.

22

I hear you bellowing in the dead of night
over the roaring sea.
And I come out to listen to you, helpless, feeling my way,
to see between the frost and
peaceful sound of growing pastures
bearing down on my still
desolation that barren land of yours,
that sand pit of dead bodies
your voice blows over those shadows.

23

(21 de junio)

Ven y que te amortaje entre violetas
en esta planetaria noche triste,
final de tantas cosas, para siempre
bajo escombros un número sangriento;

que te amortaje, sí, mientras el humo
de este otoño del sur me va borrando,
dándome alma de hoja consumida,
niebla en la niebla, sueño de otro sueño;

que la mortaja fresca que te doy
traspase de morado olor y húmeda
luz esas vivas, misteriosas ramas,
oculto pasto verde de tus huesos.
Ven y que te amortaje entre violetas.

(1940)

23

(June 21)

Come here and let me cover you with violets
this sad night of the planet,
so many things over, forever
a bloodsoaked number under rubble;

come, let me cover you, as the smoke
of autumn in the South blots me out,
leaving my soul a brown leaf,
fog in the fog, dream of another dream;

let this fresh covering
send purple odors and moist
light through those living, mysterious stems,
hidden green pasture of your bones.
Come here and let me cover you with violets.

(1940)

24

(A González Carbalho)

Amigo de la pena,
amigo, amigo:
que el dolor solo, mira,
no sea sólo tu amigo.

Mira: sólo tu amigo.

Cuando el trigal se duele,
amigo, amigo,
se duele todo el trigo.

Mira: todo el trigo.

Y si el pastor se queja,
amigo, amigo,
llora toda la aldea.

Mira: toda la aldea.

Amigo, mira el mar:
si se duele una ola,
son todas las que rompen a llorar.

Todas, mira, a llorar.
Amigo, amigo.

24

(To González Carbalho)

Friend of grief,
friend, friend:
look, sorrow alone can't be
your only friend.

Look: your only friend.

When the wheatfield grieves,
friend, friend,
all wheat grieves.

Look: all of the wheat.

When the shepherd is hurt,
friend, friend,
the whole village weeps.

Look: the whole village.

Friend, look at the sea:
if a single wave grieves,
every last one breaks into tears.

Look, everyone is crying.
Friend, friend.

25

Todos creíamos.
El mar no quiso ser mar.
(Fuimos a verlo. Era cierto.)

Todos creíamos.
La noche se ha vuelto toro.
(Fuimos a verlo. Era cierto.)

Todos creíamos.
La tierra habló y dijo: ¡Tierra!
(Fuimos a verlo. Era cierto.)

Todos creíamos.
Se hirió de muerte la muerte.
(Fuimos a verlo. Era cierto.)

Todos creíamos todo,
menos lo que hoy creemos.
(¿Será cierto?)

25

Everyone of us believed.
The sea refused to be the sea.
(We went to see for ourselves. It was true.)

Everyone of us believed.
Night became a bull.
(We went to see for ourselves. It was true.)

Everyone of us believed.
Earth spoke and said: "Land!"
(We went to see for ourselves. It was true.)

Everyone of us believed.
Death was fatally wounded.
(We went to see for ourselves. It was true.)

Everyone believed everything
but what we now believe.
(Is it true?)

26

Quiero decirte, toro, que en América,
desde donde en ti pienso—noche siempre—,
se presencian los mapas, esos grandes,
deshabitados sueños que es la Tierra.

Bien por aquí podrías, solitario
huésped y amigo, esas sedientas ascuas,
que un estoque enterrado hasta los huesos
prende en tu sangre, helarlas mansamente.

Yo quería dormir tranquilo, un poco,
pues me hace falta, como a ti; quería,
cuan largo y triste como tú, tumbarme
siquiera en el retraso de una aurora.

Pero me he levantado, ya que andaba,
párpado insomne el fijo pensamiento,
pensando en ti, para—¡luceros sordos
en la noche de América!—decírtelo.

26

I want to tell you, bull, that in America
where I think of you—always at night—
maps show up, those large
lonely dreams the Earth is.

Here, solitary guest and friend, you
could easily freeze those red-hot coals
a blade buried to the bone
fires in your blood.

I'd like to sleep soundly, a short while,
since, like you, I need to; I'd like,
stretched out and sad as you, to lie down
even if the dawn's late.

But I've gotten up, since I was,
my sleepless eyes fixed on you,
thinking of you, in order—deaf morning stars
in the night of America—to tell you so.

27

Abrí la puerta.
En donde no había camino,
vi una vereda.
Anduve.

Anduve, y a los dos lados,
bien dormido, iba sembrando:
al uno, pasto de plata;
al otro, dorado.

Cuando volvía,
como una sombra, vi un toro,
llorando.

27

I opened the door.
Where there was no road
I saw a path.
I took it.

I walked, and on both sides,
sound asleep, I began to sow:
in one, a pasture of silver;
in the other, gold.

When I returned,
like a shadow, I saw a bull,
crying.

28

Aquellos algarrobos
me oyeron cantar,
junto a la noble muerte
y el noble mar.

Pobre toro cercano,
te oigo bramar.

Algarrobos de América,
me veis llorar,
junto a la rota vida
y el nuevo andar.

Pobre toro lejano,
te oigo bramar.

28

Those carob trees
heard me singing,
by the noble death
and the noble sea.

Poor bull close by,
I hear you bellowing.

Carobs of America,
you see me crying,
by the shattered life
and the new life.

Poor bull so far away,
I hear you bellowing.

29

Cornearás aún y más que nunca,
desdoblando los campos de tu frente,
y salpicando valles y laderas
te elevarás de nuevo toro verde.

Las aldeas
perderán sus senderos para verte.

Se asomarán los hombros de los ríos,
y las espadas frías de las fuentes
manos muertas harán salir del suelo,
enramadas de júbilo y laureles.

Los ganados
perderán sus pastores para verte.

Te cantarán debajo tus dos mares,
y para ti los trigos serán puentes
por donde saltes, nuevo toro libre,
dueño de ti y de todo para siempre.

Los caminos
perderán sus ciudades para verte.

Mens non exulat.
OVIDIO.

You will gore on, now more than ever,
parting the fields of your forehead in two,
and sprinkling valleys and hillsides,
you will rise anew green bull.

Villages
will lose their footpaths to see you.

The shoulders of rivers will spring up,
and the cold swords of fountains
will draw dead hands from the ground,
bowers of joy and laurels.

Livestock
will lose their herdsmen to see you.

They will sing to you under your two seas,
and wheatfields will be bridges
you leap over, a new bull free,
your own master and master of everything forever.

Roads
will lose their cities to see you.

Mind is not exiled
OVID

5

DE LOS ÁLAMOS Y LOS SAUCES

EN RECUERDO DE ANTONIO MACHADO

> . . . *y por oílla*
> *los sauces se inclinaron a la orilla.*
> PEDRO DE ESPINOSA

> . . . *álamos de las márgenes del Duero,*
> *conmigo vais, mi corazón os lleva!*
> ANTONIO MACHADO

OF POPLARS AND WILLOWS

IN MEMORY OF ANTONIO MACHADO

> . . . *and to hear her*
> *willows leaned toward the shore.*
> PEDRO DE ESPINOSA

> . . . *poplars of the banks of the Duero,*
> *you are with me, you are in my heart!*
> ANTONIO MACHADO

11

Así como los álamos que olvidan
el desvanecimiento de los sauces;
al igual de las piedras vagabundas
que terminan de pronto en un estanque;
como la misma luz que lo sabía
y llega en un momento a no acordarse;
como la misma mano que lo escribe
y sin relampagueo se desvae;
así como esta niebla
que unifica en la nada
lo que ya no es de nadie;
así hombres, naciones,
así imperios,
estrellas,
mares...

Iba a decir, mas cuando fue a decirlo,
había muerto el lenguaje.

11

Like poplars that overlook
the fainting willows;
like wandering stones
that end abruptly in a pond;
like the very light that knew it once
and suddenly is unable to remember;
like the very hand that writes it
and in a flash trails off;
like this fog
that unites in nothingness
what no longer belongs to anyone;
so men and women, nations,
empires,
stars,
seas . . .

You were going to say, but when you went to say it,
language had died.

POEMAS DE PUNTA DEL ESTE

[1945–1956]

POEMS OF PUNTA DEL ESTE

2

EL APARECIDO

Se me aparece blanco en la mañana.
Me mira y largamente pensativo
se va girando en torno de la casa.

Luego, en el bosque, me lo encuentro verde.
Me mira, las orejas levantadas.
Suena el aire del mar. Lo aspira y lento
se va girando en torno de la casa.

Rojo, se me aparece por la tarde,
perdido en las arenas de la playa.
Arden las olas, las contempla y triste
se va girando en torno de la casa.

Se me aparece negro por la noche,
altas las crines, fija la mirada.
Sube la luna. Le relincha y solo
se va girando en torno de la casa.

2

THE GHOST

It appears to me white in the morning.
It looks at me and deeply lost in thought
goes round and round the house.

Later, in the woods, I come upon it green.
It looks at me, pricking up its ears.
The air echoes the sea. It inhales it and slowly
goes round and round the house.

It appears to me red in the afternoon,
lost in the sands of the beach.
The waves burn, it studies them and sadly
goes round and round the house.

It appears to me black at night,
staring, its mane bristling.
The moon rises. It neighs at it and alone
goes round and round the house.

6

HAN DESCUAJADO UN ÁRBOL

Han descuajado un árbol. Esta misma mañana,
el viento aún, el sol, todos los pájaros
lo acariciaban buenamente. Era
dichoso y joven, cándido y erguido,
con una clara vocación de cielo
y con un alto porvenir de estrellas.
Hoy, a la tarde, yace como un niño
desenterrado de su cuna, rotas
las dulces piernas, la cabeza hundida,
desparramado por la tierra y triste,
todo deshecho en hojas,
en llanto verde todavía, en llanto.
Esta noche saldré—cuando ya nadie
pueda mirarlo, cuando ya esté solo—
a cerrarle los ojos y a cantarle
esa misma canción que esta mañana
en su pasar le susurraba el viento.

6

THEY'VE UPROOTED A TREE

They've uprooted a tree. Only this morning
the wind, the sun and all the birds still
were simply kissing it. It was
happy and young, frank and straight,
with a clear, heavenly calling,
and a high starry future.
This afternoon, it lies like a child
dug from the cradle, the sweet
legs broken, the head sunk,
sprawled sadly on the ground,
a ruin in leaves,
in grief still green, in grief.
Tonight I'll go out—when no one
is watching, when it's all alone—
and close its eyes and sing for it
the same song the passing wind
whispered to it this morning.

7

EL BOSQUE ES GRANDE Y SOLITARIO...

El bosque es grande y solitario, vive
como encerrado dentro de una nave
de silencio tan sólo conmovido
por el propio silencio de sus hojas.
No sabe que está el cielo más arriba,
sostenido por él, por los callados
puntales de sus troncos.
Su extraña luz le brota de sí mismo.
Lo habita solamente, negro y mudo,
un caballo que a veces
hunde los ojos en el bosque y piensa:
—¿Por dónde andará hoy ese caballo
que habita solamente,
negro y mudo, este bosque?

7

THE WOODS ARE VAST AND LONELY . . .

The woods are vast and lonely and live
as though confined inside a ship
of silence moved only
by the stillness of their leaves.
They don't know the sky is above,
supported by the silent
pillars of their trunks.
From within them comes a strange light.
Only a black and silent horse
lives in there, a horse which sometimes
eyes the woods and wonders:
"Where will he be today
that black and silent horse
which lives alone in the woods?"

9

Y SIN EMBARGO, BOSQUES . . .

Y sin embargo, bosques, y sin embargo, mares,
no estamos solos, nunca
nadie está solo, sino
aquellos que están muertos de verdad en la vida,
con la sangre y los ojos y el corazón cerrados
a las profundas luces y sombras que los ciñen.
Yo os pueblo, mares, de mis cosas. Bosques,
de mis cosas también yo os pueblo. Sombras
no son. Mirad esa muchacha. Vedla
cómo marcha a mi lado entre los troncos
y sale al mar, entrándome en las olas.
Y sin embargo, bosques, y sin embargo, mares,
parecéis que estáis solos,
como yo lo parezco también hoy
tan distante de vuestros verdes ámbitos.

9

AND STILL, WOODS . . .

And still, woods, and still, seas,
we are not alone, no one
is ever alone, except
the true living dead
whose blood and eyes and heart are closed
to the profound lights and shadows around them.
I people you, seas, with my possessions. Woods,
I people you also with my things. They are not
shadows. Look at that young girl. See
how she walks by my side among the tree trunks
and enters the sea, taking me into the waves.
And still, woods, and still, seas,
you look as if you're alone,
the way I too seem alone today
so far from your green boundaries.

10

NO SE OYE EL MAR HOY EN EL BOSQUE...

Para Aitana

No se oye el mar hoy en el bosque. ¿Acaso
irrumpió en él de pronto esta mañana,
quedándose encantado,
mudo sueño de sal, entre las ramas?
Corro, inquieto, a buscarlo
antes que el bosque cierre sus ventanas
y el mar se muera sin saber ya nunca
los caminos que llevan a la playa.

10

THE SEA CAN'T BE HEARD IN THE WOODS TODAY . . .

For Aitana

The sea can't be heard in the woods today. Maybe
it burst into them this morning,
and is still in a trance,
a mute dream of salt, among the branches?
Worried, I run to find it
before the woods close their windows
and the sea dies never having known
the roads leading to the shore.

11

NO PUEDE, NO...

No puede, no, no puede la belleza
morir o ser cegada
por cualquier conmoción o cataclismo.
Ceñido estoy a veces de catástrofes,
con la patria perdida,
con mis mares y bosques allá lejos,
sin mí, desesperados.
Y sin embargo, oh tú, distante, emerges.
Venus real de espumas y de hojas.
Cuerpo de savias verdes y salitres
enamorados subes.
En él la arena teje con las ramas
altos salientes, tibias oquedades.
Dichosos los que al fin de la tormenta,
o incluso en medio de sus rojos rayos,
te suspiran, te tocan y se mueren
por ti, por ti, que eres también la aurora.

11
IT CAN'T, NO . . .

It can't, no, beauty can't
die or be blinded
by any shock or cataclysm.
I'm gripped at times by catastrophes:
my homeland lost,
my seas and woods so far away,
despairing, without me.
And still you emerge, in the distance,
true Venus of foam and leaves.
Body of green sap and loving saltpeter,
you ascend.
Sand and branches weave on it
tall peaks and warm hollows.
Happy are they who at the storm's end,
or in the midst even of its red rays,
sigh for you, touch you and die
for you, for you who are also the dawn.

12
LLOVIÓ, LLOVIÓ, LLOVIÓ...

Para Annette,
en la gracia de su adolescencia

Llovió, llovió, llovió como en otoño
llueve en los bosques junto al mar. No había
esa tarde en el bosque más que el agua
que ávidamente iba entre las hojas
bebiéndose la tierra.
De las mojadas sombras, dulces, mínimos,
sus pálidas coronas entreabrieron
los pensativos hongos infantiles.
Inmóviles, los árboles no eran
más que troncos dormidos. La muchacha
iba, tranquila, por el bosque mudo.
De pronto, un árbol la miró y sus ramas
ansiosamente descendieron... Nunca
volvió a entrar nadie más en aquel bosque.

12

IT RAINED AND RAINED, RAINED...

For Annette
in the grace of her adolescence

It rained and rained, rained like it rains
in autumn in the woods close to the sea. This afternoon
there was only water in the woods
greedily going among the leaves
drinking in the earth.
From the wet shadows, sweet and small,
the thoughtful, childlike mushrooms
half-opened their pale crowns.
The trees, still, were no more
than sleeping trunks. The young girl
went calmly through the silent woods.
Suddenly, a tree saw her and
lowered its branches longingly ... No one ever
entered these woods again.

RETORNOS
DE LO VIVO LEJANO
[1948–1956]
THE RETURN OF THE
DISTANT LIVING PAST

RETORNOS DE UN POETA ASESINADO

Has vuelto a mí más viejo y triste en la dormida
luz de un sueño tranquilo de marzo, polvorientas
de un gris inesperado las sienes, y aquel bronce
de olivo que tu mágica juventud sostenía,
surcado por el signo de los años, lo mismo
que si la vida aquella que en vida no tuviste
la hubieras paso a paso ya vivido en la muerte.

Yo no sé qué has querido decirme en esta noche
con tu desprevenida visita, el fino traje
de alpaca luminosa, como recién cortado,
la corbata amarilla y el sufrido cabello
al aire, igual que entonces
por aquellos jardines de estudiantiles chopos
y calientes adelfas.

Tal vez hayas pensado —quiero explicarme ahora
ya en las claras afueras del sueño— que debías
llegar primero a mí desde esas subterráneas
raíces o escondidos manantiales en donde
desesperadamente penan tus huesos.
                                    Dime
confiésame, confiésame
si en el abrazo mudo que me has dado, en el tierno
ademán de ofrecerme una silla, en la simple
manera de sentarte junto a mí, de mirarme,
sonreír y en silencio, sin ninguna palabra,
dime si no has querido significar con eso
que, a pesar de las mínimas batallas que reñimos,
sigues unido a mí más que nunca en la muerte
por las veces que acaso
no lo estuvimos —¡ay, perdóname!— en la vida.

Si no es así, retorna nuevamente en el sueño
de otra noche a decírmelo.

THE RETURN OF AN ASSASSINATED POET

You have come back to me older and sadder in the sleeping
light of a tranquil dream in March, your dusty
temples prematurely gray, that olive
tan your magical youth nourished,
furrowed by the passing years, as if,
in death, you lived out step by step
that life you never had in life.

I don't know what you wanted to tell me tonight
with your unexpected visit, that fine suit
of lustrous alpaca, looking like new,
that yellow tie and your dark hair uncovered,
the same as when
you walked through those gardens of student poplars
and warm oleanders.

Perhaps you thought—I want to explain myself
now that I am in the clear zone outside these dreams—that you
should come first to me from those underground
roots or hidden springs, where
your bones despair.
                  Tell me
confide in me, tell me
if in this silent embrace you've given me, in this tender
gesture of offering me a chair, in this simple
manner of sitting near me, of looking at me,
smiling and in silence, without a single word,
tell me if you did not mean
that, in spite of our squabbles,
you remain attached to me more than ever in death
for those times perhaps
we were not—oh, forgive me!—in life.

Come back again in another night's dream
and tell me if this isn't so.

BALADAS Y CANCIONES DEL PARANÁ

[1953–1954]

BALLADS AND SONGS OF THE PARANÁ

CANCIÓN 1

¡Bañado del Paraná!
Desde un balcón mira un hombre
el viento que viene y va.

Ve las barrancas movidas
del viento que viene y va.

Los caballos, como piedras
del viento que viene y va.

Los pastos, como mar verde
del viento que viene y va.

El río, como ancha cola
del viento que viene y va.

Los barcos, como caminos
del viento que viene y va.

El hombre, como la sombra
del viento que viene y va.

El cielo, como morada
del viento que viene y va.

Ve lo que mira y mirando
ve sólo su soledad.

SONG 1

Swamp of the Paraná!
A man on a balcony looks
at the wind that comes and goes.

He sees the ravines moved
of the wind that comes and goes.

The horses, as stones
of the wind that comes and goes.

The pastures, as green sea
of the wind that comes and goes.

The river, as wide tail
of the wind that comes and goes.

The ships, as roads
of the wind that comes and goes.

The man, as the shadow
of the wind that comes and goes.

The sky, as home
of the wind that comes and goes.

He sees what he looks at and looking
sees only his solitude.

CANCIÓN 4

Los barcos pasan tan cerca
de la orilla,
que bien pudieran llevarse
una rama de los sauces
de la orilla.

Está tan cerca la orilla,
que si los barcos quisieran
también pudieran llevarse
un caballo de la orilla.

¡Qué bien estar a la orilla
de esta orilla
en donde pueden los barcos,
si es que los barcos quisieran,
llevarse al mar un caballo,
una rama de los sauces
y la orilla!

SONG 4

Those ships pass so close
to the shore
they could well take
a branch from the willows
on the shore.

The shore is so close,
that ships if they wanted
could also take
a horse from the shore.

It's good to be at the edge
of the shore
where ships can,
if ships really want,
carry to sea a horse,
a branch from the willows
and the shore!

CANCIÓN 7

Basta un balcón sobre el río
y unos caballos paciendo
para viajar noche y día
sin moverse.

Los caballos están fijos
y el río está quieto siempre.
Sólo, a veces,
pasa un barco que lo inquieta,
y el aire, para moverse
un poco y trabajar algo,
cambia un caballo de sitio,
y allí lo deja.

Y el hombre del balcón vuelve,
mientras, de un largo viaje,
sin moverse.

SONG 7

A balcony over a river
and horses grazing
are enough
to travel night and day
without moving.

The horses are perfectly still
and the river is always quiet.
Once in a while
a boat passes and disturbs it.
And the air, to get moving
and do something,
nudges one of the horses over
and leaves it there.

And the man on the balcony, meanwhile,
returns from a long trip,
without moving.

BALADA DEL ANDALUZ PERDIDO

Perdido está el andaluz
del otro lado del río.

—Río, tú que lo conoces:
¿quién es y por qué se vino?

Vería los olivares
cerca tal vez de otro río.

—Río, tú que lo conoces:
¿qué hace siempre junto al río?

Vería el odio, la guerra,
cerca tal vez de otro río.

—Río, tú que lo conoces:
¿qué hace solo junto al río?

Veo su rancho de adobe
del otro lado del río.

No veo los olivares
del otro lado del río.

Sólo caballos, caballos,
caballos, solos, perdidos.

¡Soledad de un andaluz
del otro lado del río!

¿Qué hará solo ese andaluz
del otro lado del río?

BALLAD OF THE LOST ANDALUSIAN

Lost is the Andalusian
on the other side of the river.

"River, you who know him:
who is he and why has he come?"

Perhaps he has seen olive groves
beside some other river.

"River, you who know him:
what does he do forever by the river?"

Perhaps he has seen hate, war,
beside some other river?

"River, you who know him:
what does he do alone by the river?"

I see his adobe hut
on the other side of the river.

I do not see olive groves
on the other side of the river.

Only horses, horses,
horses, alone, lost.

Solitude of an Andalusian
on the other side of the river!

What will this one Andalusian do
on the other side of the river?

CANCIÓN 16

(Antonio Machado)

Con cuánta melancolía
pienso en ti. Tú hubieras visto
lo que yo miro esta tarde.
Cosas naturales, cosas
tan buenas, puras y santas,
que sólo pueden mirarse
con lágrimas en los ojos.
Un río que no se mueve,
pero que nos da la mano,
susurrando nuestro nombre.
Un caballo que levanta,
al vernos pasar, la frente,
queriéndonos decir algo.
Un perro fiel que nos prueba
su amor y su mansedumbre
durmiéndose a nuestras plantas.
Un árbol que nos ofrece
su sombra como el amigo
que nos entrega su casa.
Y una pradera encendida
que llega hasta el horizonte,
tendiendo pastos tranquilos
en el cielo...

SONG 16

(Antonio Machado)

I think of you
with such sadness. You should have seen
what I'm seeing this afternoon.
Natural things, things
so good, holy and pure
they can only be looked at
through tears.
A river perfectly still,
that shakes our hand
and murmurs our name.
A horse raising its head
to see us pass,
to tell us something.
A faithful dog showing
its love and gentleness
by sleeping at our feet.
A tree offering us
shade like a friend
taking us into his home.
And a meadow on fire
reaching to the horizon,
spreading still pastures
in the sky . . .

CANCIÓN 39

Las velas ya derramaron
cuantas lágrimas tenían.
No tienen más que llorar.
Empiezo a ver. Me acompaña
tan sólo la oscuridad.

La más viva oscuridad.

SONG 39

The candles have shed
every tear they had.
They can't cry anymore.
I begin to see. Darkness
is my only company.

The burning darkness.

CANCIÓN 40

No volvieron. Y yo estoy triste.
Triste el bañado, sin Aitana.

Un caballo la espera, solo.
Me quiere hablar.
                    —Vendrá mañana.

No volvieron. Y yo estoy triste.
Tristes los ríos, sin Aitana.

Un velero la espera, solo.
Me quiere hablar.
                    —Vendrá mañana.

(Digo yo que vendrá mañana.)

SONG 40

They didn't return. And I am sad.
The swamp is sad, without Aitana.

A horse waits for her, alone.
It wants to tell me something.
      "She'll come tomorrow."

They didn't return. And I am sad.
The rivers are sad, without Aitana.

A sailboat waits for her, alone.
It wants to tell me something.
      "She'll come tomorrow."

(I tell you she'll come tomorrow.)

CANCIÓN 49

Aquel río, un mediodía,
se volvió duro, de acero.
Barcos que por él pasaban,
no volvieron.
El viento, sí, sólo el viento.

El viento furioso, a golpes,
para romperlo.
Con la cabeza y el pecho.
Día y noche,
con la cabeza y el pecho.

Pero aquel río era un río
de acero.
Ya, para siempre, de acero.

SONG 49

There was a river
that one noon
turned hard, into steel.
Boats that traveled it
never returned.
Only the wind did, only the wind.

To break it
the angry wind hammered it with blows.
With its head and with its chest.
Day and night,
with its head and with its chest.

But the river was a river
of steel.
Now, and forever, of steel.

CANCIÓN 16

Cuando estoy solo, me salen
coplas nada más, coplillas
que no le importan ni al aire.
Hoy que solo me he quedado,
sin ni siquiera mirarme,
el aire pasó de largo.

SONG 16

When I am alone, only a few
lines come out, lines so slight
even the air ignores them.
Today when I was left alone,
the air passed me by,
without so much as a nod.

CANCIÓN 39

Sol de esta tierra, yo llevo,
de otra tierra, un sol adentro.

Aquí está el tuyo, aquí el mío,
frente a frente, pero idénticos.

Me hace arder el tuyo, el mío
me hace siempre estar ardiendo.

Dos soles me están quemando.
Yo soy un toro de fuego.

SONG 39

Sun of this earth, I carry,
from another earth, a sun inside.

Here is yours, here is mine,
face to face, but exactly alike.

Yours makes me burn, mine
keeps me constantly on fire.

Two suns are consuming me.
I am a bull on fire.

CANCIÓN 35

Pienso ahora—medianoche—
que nunca dormí en la vida,
que cerré de cuando en cuando
los ojos y sumergía
en la apariencia del sueño,
sin dormir, cuando veía.

SONG 35

I think now—at midnight—
that I never slept in my life,
that when from time to time I closed
my eyes and submerged all I saw
in the semblance of sleep,
I didn't sleep.

CONTRIBUTORS NOTES

José A. Elgorriaga is chairman of the Department of Foreign Languages at California State University in Fresno. He was born in Spain and as a boy emigrated with his parents to California.

Martin Paul, also at California State University in Fresno, teaches in the English Department. With José Elgorriaga he is working on translations of the work of Antonio Machado.

Gabriel Berns is professor of Spanish Literature at the University of California, Santa Cruz. His translation of Alberti's autobiography, *La arboleda perdida (The Lost Grove)* was published in 1976. He now lives in San Francisco.

Kosrof Chantikian lives and works in San Francisco. His second book of poems, *Prophecies & Transformations,* appeared in 1978. He edited *Octavio Paz: Homage to the Poet,* published by *KOSMOS* in 1981.